THE MINISTER AS PROPHET

BY

CHARLES EDWARD JEFFERSON

PASTOR OF THE BROADWAY TABERNACLE
IN NEW YORK CITY

NEW YORK
THOMAS Y. CROWELL & CO.
PUBLISHERS

COPYRIGHT, 1905,
BY THOMAS Y. CROWELL & CO.

PUBLISHED MARCH, 1905.

THE GEORGE SHEPARD
LECTURES ON PREACHING

At Bangor Theological Seminary

1904–1905

CONTENTS

I

THE MINISTER AS PROPHET

I

The Dimensions of the Work

A MINISTER of the Gospel is expected to do a wider variety of things than any other man in the community. The division of labor has been carried farther in every other profession than in the ministry. His work is multiform, and it is impossible in five brief lectures to cover more than a small fraction of it.

The minister is an administrator. His church is an organization, and like all organizations it must have an executive head. The minister is that head. It is in one sense a machine, and like all machines must be run. Friction must be reduced, the wheels must be lubricated, repairs must be made, every part of the

mechanism must be subjected to constant
scrutiny and supervision, in order that
the machine may do the work for which
it has been created. The work of administration is of great importance, but
into that kingdom we cannot enter now.

The minister is a pastor, a shepherd
of the flock. He must tend and feed
the sheep. He must know them all by
name, and he must know also their dispositions, needs, and habits, and knowing
these he must be acquainted with the
pastures where the grass is greenest and
most abundant, and he must know where
the most refreshing waters flow, and he
must know the character and the methods
of the enemies by which the flock is most
likely to be attacked. The work of shep-
herding is of vast concern, but into this
province we cannot go.

The minister is a priest; he officiates
at the altar of worship. He is the spokesman of the people as they offer up their
sacrifice of praise and prayer. He leads

the congregation to the throne of grace. Upon his lips the desires and thoughts of many hearts become vocal. He reads the scriptures, interpreting by emphasis and intonation the revelation which has come through holy men of old. While he does not lead the singing, it is for him to decide what shall be the character and amount of the music in which the church shall express its adoration and thanksgiving. He is the ordained ministrant in the service in which the Lord's people bear public testimony to their faith, and to him is intrusted the entire conduct of worship in the house of prayer. It is a critical and difficult work, but into this wide region we cannot make our way.

The minister is a moral and religious leader. As a guide he has relations not only to his own congregation, but to the entire denomination of which he is a representative, and to the church universal of which he is a member, and not only does he have relations to organized Christianity,

but he is related to the great philanthropic and reformatory movements of
his age, and belongs in a special sense to
the entire community in the midst of
which he does his work.   All these relations bring with them unescapable obliga-
tions and multitudinous duties.   The work
of minister as patriot and citizen is one
of far-reaching influence and significance,
but from all this territory we are for the
time shut out.

The minister is a prophet of the Lord.
By prophet is meant a man who speaks
for God.   He is preëminently a speaker.
His business is to speak for another.   He
is a truth-teller, and therefore first of all a
truth-seeker.   He must dig for it as for
hidden treasures, and having found it, he
must coin it and put it into circulation
among the people.   Like a Moses, he must
go up into the mountain and talk with God
face to face, coming down and giving to
his brethren his latest revelation.   He is a
missionary intrusted with the good news,

and he must speak his message without diminution or any blurring of its contents. He is an ambassador sent from the court of heaven to the court of earth, and his life is one long and passionate appeal to men to become reconciled to God.

This work of speaking for God is only a part of the modern minister's duty, but it is a realm of such wide dimensions that we shall be justified in confining our attention exclusively to it. But in passing over all the other departments of ministerial activity and shutting ourselves up with preaching alone, I would not have any one of you think that these other forms of work hold in my mind a place of comparative unimportance, or that in my judgment a minister can shirk all his duties but that of preaching and still accomplish the work which God has given him to do. If time allowed, I could speak for five evenings on each branch of work to which reference has been made, and still be unable to say all that can reasonably be said about their

importance to a minister who wishes to
be a workman that needeth not to be
ashamed.

My ground for directing your attention
especially to preaching is not because I
underestimate the other forms of ministerial duty, or because I would have you
ignore them in your own thought and
work; but because there are just now several special reasons why a minister of the
Gospel should give himself with renewed
zeal to the great work of preaching. The
considerations which have led me thus to
limit the scope of these lectures are: —

1. The work of preaching is the most
difficult of all the things which a minister
is called to do. Indeed, it is the most
difficult task to which any mortal can set
himself. It is at once the most strenuous
and the most exacting of all forms of labor.
It requires a fuller combination of faculties
and a finer balance of powers than are required in any other department of human
effort. It is a difficult thing to paint a

portrait. To gain the skill required to place the features of the human face on the canvas in such a way as that they shall breathe and speak requires the unflagging toil of years, but how much more difficult it is with human words to paint the face of Christ so that he shall woo and win the hearts of men.

It is a difficult thing to master the mysteries of the world of tone, and create harmonies and melodies which will set the nerves a-tingling, but much more difficult it is to catch the music of the world eternal and translate it into human speech so that human hearts on which it falls shall give back the same celestial vibrations. It is a great thing to chisel the marble into forms which seem alive, but immeasurably more difficult it is to chisel character by means of words into forms which will please the King. It is a difficult thing to act upon the stage, to interpret adequately the lines of the masters of the drama. One of the greatest living actors,

now over seventy years of age, says that
he began to study the art of acting when
a boy of three, and that he is studying it
still. But how much more study and practice is required for the right rendering to
human hearts of the thoughts and purposes
of God. The lawyer has a difficult work.
It is hard to apply human law to all the
tangled and complicated affairs of men,
but to apply the law is not half so difficult
as it is to apply the Gospel. The work of
the physician is arduous, and without skill
and knowledge he is nothing ; but to minister to a mind sin-sick, to soothe a conscience crying out in pain, "to pluck from
the memory a rooted sorrow" and "raze
out the written troubles of the brain" and
"cleanse the stuff'd bosom of that perilous
stuff which weighs upon the heart"—this
requires a skill and knowledge and wisdom
and power greater than any which the
doctors know. Because the work of
preaching is so difficult is my first reason
for speaking to you about nothing else.

2. But notwithstanding the work is above all others difficult, ministers are just now in danger of receiving less help in mastering the art of preaching than in learning any other form of work. Fresh emphasis is being placed on the work of administration. With the increasing complexity of human life the church as a machine is becoming more and more intricate. Social and industrial problems are at the front, and expert hands seem to be more needed than instructive tongues. The minister's study has fallen into the background, and the minister's office is the place in which he is expected to do his work. In a commercial age it is assumed that a clergyman must have the knack of doing things, and the business aspect of religion is the one which is uppermost in the public mind.

Along with this new emphasis on administration there is fresh interest in ceremonialism. Our forms of worship are discovered to be altogether too colorless and too bare to suit a generation which

has developed all the nerves of taste, and
so men are discussing everywhere the
advisability of enriching the forms of service.   There is a widespread feeling that
the forms must be more stately, dignified,
and elaborate, and that the advantages of
a liturgy without its dangers are within
the reach of every church.   But with this
increased emphasis on the value and place
of liturgy there is a slackening sense in
many quarters of the value of the sermon.
As music increases the sermon decreases,
and many a student for the ministry is to-
day more concerned about the ordering of
worship than about the creation of effective
sermons.

Even in our seminaries, which are in
theory schools in which men are trained
to preach, the multiplication of new and
fascinating studies has had a tendency
to throw homiletics into the shade.   Ar-
chæology, historical criticism, and sociology have but recently come to their best
estate, and the worlds which they bring to

our attention are so vast and stimulating
and important that it is not to be wondered
at that many a student is far more interested in the latest results of criticism and
research than in the art of presenting New
Testament ideas in such a way as to open
the springs of the heart and turn the
streams of conduct into new channels.

Moreover, there is a widespread feeling
that preaching as an institution is more or
less obsolescent. Sermons, men say, have
had their day. Just as our national Con-
gress has ceased to be the arena for interesting and instructive debate, so the
Christian pulpit has ceased to be a center
to which men look for either instruction or
for uplift. And so the preacher is in disrepute. Coleridge once said that in " older
times writers were looked up to as inter-
mediate beings between angels and men;
afterwards they were regarded as venerable and perhaps inspired teachers; subse-
quently they descended to the level of
learned and instructive friends; but in

modern days they are deemed culprits more than benefactors."

A similar process has been going on in the public mind concerning preachers. Once they were more than human, then supremely human, later on interesting and useful, but more recently they are regarded in many sections of society as impertinences and bores. The opinion of the world cannot fail to influence the thought and feeling of ministers themselves. It is not uncommon to hear ministers speak in disparaging and apologetic tones about their sermons. And even though they say nothing slightingly with their lips, the place which they give the sermon in their thought and preparation reveals only too clearly that they have lost their faith in its importance and their ambition to make it what a sermon ought to be. Rome was near her fall when the priests who ministered at her altars joked about the mass. It is a sign of skepticism and decadence in the Protestant pulpit that so many ministers can joke about their sermons and listen to attacks upon the work of preaching without indignant protest or swift rebuke.

3. The greatest danger confronting the church of Christ in America to-day is a possible decadence of the pulpit. Let the pulpit decay, and the cause of Christ is lost. Nothing can take the place of preaching. There is no power under heaven equal to the power of a God-inspired pulpit. Anthems and hymns, responsive readings and creed recitations, prayers written and prayers extempore, all have their place, and when rightly used are means of grace; but all of them put together cannot take the place of the exposition of God's word by a man whose lips have been touched by a coal from off God's altar. An ignorant pulpit is the worst of all scourges. An ineffective pulpit is the most lamentable of all scandals. The cause of Christ is hopelessly handicapped and blocked when Christian preachers forget how

to preach.   We must guard the pulpit
with all diligence, for out of it are the
issues of life.   Any signs of decay in it
must fill all well-wishers of the church
with regret and alarm.

And history will not allow us to escape
the fact that it is easy for the pulpit to
decay.   The prophet has always had a
tendency to degenerate into the priest.
The man who speaks for God is always
prone to slip down into the man who
performs ceremonies for God.   The altitudes on which the prophet of the Lord
must live are so lofty that poor, frail
human nature, finding it exhausting to
breathe the difficult air, seeks the first
opportunity to come down.   But every
time the prophet degenerates into a priest
a new darkness falls upon the world.
There were great prophets in Israel in
Elijah's day and in Isaiah's day and in
Haggai's day, but little by little the light
of prophecy died down, the men who
spoke for God became interested in in-

cense and burnt offerings, and when the last of the prophets departed, darkness fell on Palestine.

The Christian church began in a blaze of glory — in the glory that burst from a sermon. For a season the church had great preachers, — Tertullians and Chrysostoms, Augustines and Ambroses, — but gradually the prophetic fire died down, instead of the preacher there was only the priest, and the world was in darkness again. The Reformation was ushered in by a mighty preacher, — Martin Luther, — a man educated to be a priest, but who, by the grace of God, grew to the stature of a preacher. So long as Luther and Calvin and Latimer and Knox, and the mighty men who came after them, kept the pulpit fires burning, the world rolled more and more into light, and it was daybreak everywhere. But when the preachers slid down into pedants, there was darkness once more on the earth.

England in the eighteenth century was dead, and it was a preacher — John Wesley — who raised the dead and ushered in a new epoch of Christian history. Has not America had the same experience? Did we not start with Cotton and Hooker and Shepard and Eliot and the Mathers, and did not the people who sat in the shadow of great hardships see a wonderful light? And when the light faded, it was because the great preachers were dead; and there was no life and no light in New England till an Englishman, George Whitefield, and an American, Jonathan Edwards, stood in the pulpit, like anointed princes of God, and spoke once more to the people, in burning accents, the message of redemption. The bones in the valley of death have always taken to themselves flesh and stood erect on their feet, and the water has always gushed out of the rock, and new heavens have always bent over a new earth whenever and wherever a man has appeared who was able to convert the pulpit into a throne.

4. If this is the great danger of the Christian church, then we know what is its great need. The churches, from the Atlantic to the Pacific, are crying out for preachers. It is a question often debated whether there is a call for more ministers; but however that may be, there is no doubt that there is an ever increasing demand for more preachers. Why do churches with fifty or one hundred applicants for their pulpit wait for months and sometimes for years before they can find the man they want? It is sometimes because in the whole crowd of applicants there is not one man who knows how to preach. No man who knows how to preach with grace and power need stand idle in the market-place a single hour. Churches are scouring the country in search of such a man, and he cannot escape if he would. Throughout my entire ministerial career I have been receiv-

ing almost every month, and sometimes
every week, letters from church committees asking, " Do you know a man whom
you can recommend to us for our pulpit?" And the churches which ask such
a question are, as a rule, the large and
influential churches at the center of great
populations, where strength and ability
are needed and where weaklings can avail
nothing.

Church committees, when the time
comes to select a minister, simply stand
dumfounded and baffled, unable sometimes for months to find a man with the
ability and training sufficient to make
him a power in the pulpit. The great
universities and the great railroads and
the great banks and the great business
houses and the great industrial enterprises
find it easier to secure capable men to
carry on their work than do our important
churches in securing men equal to the
demands of the modern pulpit. The age
demands men of power. And unless we

can get men for the pulpit as brainy and
competent, as versatile and resourceful, as
virile and effective, as the great captains
of industry and the merchant princes, the
church will be handicapped in her labor
and the ungodly will have fresh occasion
to blaspheme.

There are more great openings in the
Christian church for men of genuine
ability than in any other department of
our modern world. But only strong men
are equal to the problem. The work
of the preacher is to-day more difficult far than it was in the days of our
fathers, and it is growing more arduous
and taxing all the time. It will be more
difficult in twenty years from now than it
is to-day. The world is growing increasingly luxurious. Wealth is piling itself up
in glittering heaps. The world has never
been so comfortable and cozy as it is
now, and it will be still more comfortable
a quarter of a century farther on. With
life on earth increasingly delightful, it will

be increasingly difficult to lift men's eyes
to the glory of the things which are invisible and eternal. John Bunyan's man with
the muck-rake would not look up because
he was engaged in raking together sticks
and straws, but the man to whom we
preach is raking gold and precious stones ;
and who is strong enough to lift his eyes
to the celestial crown ? Life is increasingly crowded. There never have been so
many papers and books, and songs and
concerts, and entertainments and lectures
and plays, and clubs and societies and
social duties as now. Never have there
been so many things to play at or to work
with ; never so many ways to make
money and to lose money ; never so many
teachers who are ready to entertain, instruct, or inspire.

The minister is in a crowd, and he
must make room for himself or he is
lost. The cities are growing all the
time, their populations becoming more
heterogeneous, their problems more com-

plicated, their interests more multifarious, their burdens heavier, their needs more urgent, and their perils more alarming. The art of living together is a great and fine art, and to teach men how to do this requires a saint and a sage. The evils of our day are all monsters, and only a Hercules in whose heart is the spirit of Christ can face them and vanquish them. The level of culture is rising year by year. Streams of young people pour out of our universities, academies, and schools, and the graduates of these schools have a taste which must not be offended, and powers of thinking which must not be ignored. Bunglers in language and blunderbusses in the art of thinking cannot expect to catch and hold the attention of the rising generation. The man who is to preach the unsearchable riches of Christ to culti-vated congregations must be a man of native force and superb equipment.

5. What an opportunity is thus afforded to the theological seminary for making

itself a factor in the civilization of our
century ! Its supreme work is the training
of preachers. It is first of all a school of
the prophets. Whatever else it may do it
must do this, or it fails to do the one thing
essential. That it should be even sus-
pected of being negligent in pursuing its
supreme work is little less than a calamity.
The seminaries have for two decades been
the target for unlimited criticism. Sometimes the criticism has been discriminating,
and at other times it has degenerated into
almost brutal abuse. The arraignment has
been varied in the mouth of different ac-
cusers. Sometimes it has been the professors who have been cudgeled, sometimes
it has been the curriculum which has been
denounced, sometimes scornful things
have been said of the caliber of the men
who have presented themselves as students. But whatever the form of the
criticism, the root of it runs down into the
fact that our seminaries for some reason or
other do not seem to be able to supply

the churches with preachers. The graduates are in many cases fine scholars, lin-
guistic experts, church specialists, good
for professors' chairs and for the work of
research, but not effective in the pulpit
as preachers of the word.

It is surprising how stoutly and stub-
bornly the churches insist upon preachers knowing how to preach. They will
forgive almost everything else, but they
will not forgive inability to preach. They
have a wholesome reverence for learning,
but they would rather have a man with
no diploma who can preach than a man
with two diplomas who cannot preach.
They believe in experience, and acknowledge its value; but they would rather
have a man with no experience who
can preach than a man with years of
experience who has lost the gift of presenting truth in ways which lift and
strengthen. In all this the churches may
be stiff-necked and unreasonable, but it
is a frame of mind which is not likely to

be changed.   And if I were the president of a theological seminary, I should listen to what the spirit is saying through the churches, and should set my house in order for the training of preachers.   Every professor in the faculty should be chosen with an eye on the question, Will he fit men to preach? and every study in the curriculum should be there only on condition that it assisted men to preach.   I should have courses in theology, for theology is the queen of the sciences, and without theology a preacher is not equipped for his work.

But along with theology I should multiply the courses of study which deal with the problems of presenting thought in such ways as shall reach the reason and the emotions and influence the will.   The science of logic, and the science of debate, and the science of rhetoric, and the science of elocution, should all have high places, higher than have been given them hitherto. And in addition to the regular professors I should want every month some recognized pulpit leader to come into personal touch with my students, and also some great criminal lawyer who has proved indisputably by his triumphs that he can by an argument influence the thoughts and decisions of men.

There should be no stronger argument or mightier appeal heard anywhere than that which goes forth from the Christian pulpit. That men should Sunday after Sunday stand in Christian pulpits, ignorant of the fundamental rules of thinking, and utterly incompetent to use the English language with either grace or power, is a scandal of such huge dimensions that every seminary in the land ought to consecrate itself afresh to the great task of putting an end to the scandal, and training up a race of preachers who shall be able to clothe in fitting form the heavenly message intrusted to their lips.

6. Here then, brethren, is a wide door and effectual, and I appeal to you to go in. Whatever else you want to be, take a vow

that you will first of all be preachers. It is a tragic thing to be a feeble and ineffective preacher. To speak for half an hour on the Lord's day to a company of intelligent and hungry-hearted people and create no atmosphere, make no impression, lift no soul nearer heaven, this is something of which a man ought to be ashamed and for which he ought to repent in sackcloth and ashes. You have no right to disgrace yourself and degrade the pulpit by a sermon which does nothing. If you cannot start at a definite point and move onward with steadfast foot toward a well-defined goal, and stop there when you have once arrived, you do not have sufficient mental discipline to warrant you to think that God has called you to be a preacher. You cannot afford to do a stupid and ineffective thing in the pulpit. You owe it to your brother ministers to do your best. If you preach poorly, you make it harder for all your brethren to gain a hearing. You owe it to your profession to contribute your best in order that your profession may be advanced.

All of us suffer from the boobies and blunderers who have gone before us. It has become a proverb "dull as a sermon," "prosaic as a parson," and there is a prejudice in the public mind against preaching which would have been less intense and more readily removed had it not been for the sickly twaddle and the unctious exhortation which has so often been palmed off under the name of preaching. If you by your slipshod preaching create a bias against the pulpit, you not only fail to enter the kingdom of power yourself, but you prevent others from going in. Your failure involves not only yourself, but it subtracts from the influence of preachers everywhere. For the sake of your brethren in the ministry aim to preach as well as you can. And for the sake of the people to whom you as a messenger are sent, you ought to be willing never to do less than your best.

Men and women judge Christianity largely from sermons. If you make your sermons dull, then religion becomes dull also. If you present Christ in such a way that he does not attract, then you help men to fix themselves in unbelief. The worship of God will become to men a tedious and irksome thing, unless you can fill it with life drawn from the fountains of your own heart. You never know what damage you do by the preaching of a weak and worthless sermon. And in all your congregation there are no ears so sensitive and so critical as are the ears of a boy. You may have a church in which there is no millionaire, no professor, no author or painter or orator or scholar, no man or woman of cultivation or social prestige, but you will never be the pastor of a church in which there is not a boy, and that boy ought to be your salvation. On entering your pulpit, say to yourself, "There is a lad here," and for his sake if not for your own you must preach well. How many thousands of men are hopelessly estranged from the Christian church and her services because in the days of their boyhood they listened to sermons which were shallow and cheap, only the final Judgment will declare. A boy's impressions are deep, and when once made no subsequent preacher is likely to efface them.

Sir Walter Scott was all through his life biased against the Evangelical branch of the Christian church, because when a boy he had listened to the ranting of a number of ignorant and bigoted evangelists. Augustine was the son of a Christian mother, but his mother prayed for him thirty years apparently in vain. Her son was interested in philosophy and philosophers, and one of them, Faustus, had a mighty influence over him. The church had no attraction for him. Her music and her ceremonies did not appeal to him. Her officiating priests were not so interesting as the philosophers.

But by and by Augustine found his way
to Milan, and in the cathedral there behold,
a man! Ambrose. Like a prophet of the
Lord he stood there in the pulpit expound-
ing the scriptures in tones which fell on
human hearts like flakes of fire. Augustine listened, pondered, began to read the
scriptures. The old familiar words of
Jesus and the apostles began to open,
unsuspected meanings came into view, and
thus through the personality of a preacher
Augustine found his way to God. He
lived to become one of the giants of the
church of Christ, and of all men born of
women since the days of Saul of Tarsus,
not one has surpassed him in the width of
his influence or in the enduring splendor
of his fame. He was saved to the Christian church by a man in the pulpit.

What future saint of God may sit in
boys' clothing in your congregation you
cannot know; but the fact that somewhere among your hearers there may be
a boy who by his faith may transform

the life of cities or the policy of state, should lead you to make unceasing efforts to make yourself the most effective preacher which a man of your native gifts and acquired graces can in the Providence of God become.

How can you do it? Only by having faith. It is in preaching as in every other form of Christian service, the secret of our power is faith. If a man has faith as a grain of mustard seed, he can perform wonders both in the pulpit and out of it. No one can preach well who does not believe in preaching. He must believe that it is a divine institution and that it is accompanied by supernatural power. He must grasp St. Paul's deep-rooted conviction that it has pleased God to save the world by the foolishness of preaching.

The voice for which the preacher is to listen always is the Master's voice, saying, "Go preach the Gospel," and hearing this the voices of the world will not disconcert nor make afraid. The world is always doing its best to discourage preachers. The devil would rather have a minister do anything else than preach a sermon. He will persuade him if possible not to preach at all, and if he fails in this he will coax him to preach poorly. There is nothing that the powers of darkness fear and hate like the light which bursts from a genuinely Christian sermon. The world is filled with voices pleading with men not to preach. They say that the days for preaching are gone forever, that the printing-press has come, that society does not need instruction or guidance from the pulpit, for other teachers have arisen to fill the preacher's place. But to all such voices let our answer be, The printing-press is lifeless, it is made of iron and steel, and nothing without a throbbing heart can soothe and heal the hearts of men. So long as hearts are human, and so long as tongues know how to speak, the hungry heart will listen to a tongue which has learned the story of Jesus and his love. The day of preaching has not gone; it has only fairly begun. The great days of the pulpit are in front of us, and the world is groaning and travailing in pain together until now, waiting for the coming of new sons of pulpit power.

The world keeps twitting the minister on the loss of his professional prestige. He is no longer on a pedestal. He is not now the most conspicuous personage in all the town. And to all this the answer is, What of it? He never belonged upon a pedestal. That was not his place. The world gave and the world has taken away, and the minister is where he was at the beginning,—a servant of the Lord. Jesus was not on a pedestal, and it is enough for the disciple to be as his Master and the servant as his Lord. No man looms up to-day in any of the kingdoms of life as men loomed several decades ago. There is no statesman so conspicuous as Daniel Webster, no editor

so famous as Horace Greeley, no merchant so much talked of as A. T.
Stewart, and nowhere in the world is
there a teacher who has the reputation
once possessed by Gamaliel.

But to be conspicuous is not so great as
to be useful, and has the time now arrived
when the minister can be of no service
to men? Is no one needed to comfort
women in the agony over the grave of
their first born, to encourage men who,
harassed by business cares, know not how
to endure, to strengthen young men who
are fighting with passions fiercer than the
beasts of Ephesus, and to brace the
trembling hearts of those who are passing into the valley where the deep shad-
ows lie? What right has a minister to
covet a pedestal? Let him stand on the
ground by the side of his brethren!

Listen not to the world and listen not
to the despondent voices of your own
discouraged heart. Often you will be
tempted to accept the view that men are

little more than animals, and that the prevailing forces in their life are sordid and materialistic. There are eloquent descriptions of the world representing it as a world in which faith is dying and aspiration dead, inhabited by men who have lost out of their hearts the hopes of nobler times and who are asphyxiated in an atmosphere filled with spiritual poison. The man who doubts the dignity and divinity of human nature cannot reach. Banish every doubt concerning man as you would banish doubt concerning God. Meet men always on high ground. Speak to them as though they were indeed the sons of God. Have faith in God, and also have faith in man. Go out to meet men on the lofty levels on which Jesus walked in the upper chamber and in the sermon on the mount, and you will never lack an audience, and never speak in vain.

Pay no attention to your heart when it mourns over the fact that there are no results. Appearances are usually deceiving, and never so deceiving as in the field in which the preacher does his work. Little is said about sermons to the preacher. Few of his parishioners ever take the trouble to thank him for any of his sermonic work. They come, listen, and go home, silent on the sermon and on what it has accomplished for their soul. Moreover, the results cannot easily be seen. The preacher strains his eyes to find them, but they are invisible. Men seem to remain just what they were in spite of all his labor. But a minister should walk by faith and not by sight. If men do not praise him for his sermons, let him seek the honor which comes from God only. If he cannot see the results of his work, let him remember that spiritual harvests are slow in coming, and that his will grow golden in some far-off autumn sun.

Lyman Beecher, preaching on the sovereignty of God, did not know that young Wendell Phillips was in his congregation; nor did he know that after the benediction Wendell Phillips hurried to his room, threw himself on his knees, and dedicated himself for life to the service of the King. Newman Hall did not know that during one of his sermons a poor, obscure seamstress was converted by his words. It was at the end of twenty years that she sent him a bouquet as a token of gratitude for the peace of God which had come to her through him. The humble preacher in Ecclefechan never dreamed that little Tommy Carlyle would some day be one of England's foremost men of letters, and would say, referring to the early sermons, "The mark of that man is on me!" No man ever knows what he is accomplishing when he works with ideas and human souls. It is enough to know that he who works with truth and life never works without results, and that he who works with God works with one who has said, "My word shall not re-

turn unto me void, but it shall accomplish
that which I please, and it shall prosper
in the thing whereto I sent it."

Be of good cheer, therefore, and remember you stand in the line of a great
succession. Think often of the giants
who have preceded you in this work.
Read what they did, and revel in their
triumphs. Surrounded by so great a
cloud of witnesses who have received
their crowns, you will offer a more steadfast testimony and abound in the work of
the Lord till the end of the day. It is
well to remember also the saying of a
Puritan preacher, Thomas Goodwin, "God
had only one son, and he made him a
minister."

II

The Three Men Involved

IT takes three men to preach a sermon,
— the physical man, the mental man, and
the spiritual man. Let us give these
three men our attention.

1. *The Physical Man.* We are just
beginning to understand the body. It is
dawning upon us that it is really a part
of man, not an adjunct or an after-
thought, but an integral part of his
being. The mediæval conception of the
flesh has dominated the world almost
to the present generation. In theory we
threw that conception away long ago, but
much of our thinking and more of our
practice have been unconsciously colored
and molded by it. Many a man even
in our day has acted in student days and

afterward as though he were a spirit only, and had no body to which any thought was due. But we are coming to see that the body is no less divine than the soul, and that without a body man is not man, either in this world or in any other. He is not body alone, neither is he soul only, but he is soul and body; the two together make the man. Without the body the soul can do nothing on this earth, and therefore the study of the body and the care for its development are as indispensable in every rational system of education as is attention devoted to the soul. A minister cannot preach without his body, and, other things being equal, the sounder his body, the more effective will be his preaching.

Indeed, the body is more implicated in the work of the preacher than in the work of many a man who seems to use his body only. A minister is subjected to a nervous strain which is continuous, and which at times becomes terrific. Heavy weights hang on all his nerve centers. As an administrator he is called upon to do work which is taxing to a degree. It is easy to work with sticks and stones, for they are without life and will stay where they are put. It is easy to work with shrubs and flowers, for having no emotions of their own they do not lose their temper or come into conflict with those who strive to train them. Shrubs and flowers, however, have life, and having life they have habits and inclinations, and therefore the horticulturist has more to think about and watch, and meets with greater disappointments than the man who works with matter which is dead.

When one works with animals a greater degree of attention is required, for in animals there are emotions and passions, and these are constantly coming into collision with the will of those who would manage them. It requires a greater alertness of mind and a firmer patience to deal with oxen, horses, mules, than are required in the successful management of trees and flowers. But when we come to human beings, we find life in all its fullness, with appetites, passions, dispositions, inclinations, and a will which must be trained to work in harmony with other wills. The crudenesses and limitations and perversities of human nature are incalculable, and to keep several hundred men and women in one household of faith living and working harmoniously together requires an alertness, a resourcefulness, and a patience which often leave the heart fatigued.

But this is not more exhausting than is the work of the pastor. A minister has with him always the poor, the sick, the bereaved, the dying, the forlorn, and broken. None of these is it possible for him to escape. He must bear their burdens on his heart. He must touch them, and every time he touches them strength goes from him. To be a successful preacher a man must be finely organized, but no man can have a sensitive organization without responding

to the want and woe of the people whose
lives are pressed close against his own. A
half hour in the sick chamber may be
more exhausting than ten hours of manual
labor, and one funeral may leave a man
sapped and jaded for a day. Men who
think the minister has an easy life do not
know what it is to be a pastor. His work
as priest is by no means easy. To carry a
congregation to the throne of grace is one
of the most taxing of all labors to any man
who realizes what public worship really is.

There is not a moment in the service
when a true priest's heart is not radiating
life and heat, and with some men the out-
flow of vitality through scripture reading
and extemporaneous prayer is so tremendous that they are well-nigh exhausted before the time for preaching has arrived. To
conduct public worship as public worship
ought to be conducted is a joy which only
the redeemed can know, but it is a joy
which must be paid for with blood. In
his outside work as patriot and citizen the

engagements are numerous and the burdens are heavy. The minister must on
many occasions voice the sentiments and
convictions of the public, and whenever he
speaks he must speak in such a way as to
do justice to himself and honor to those
whose spokesman he is.

But it is in the work of preaching that
we come to the heaviest tax and the
severest strain on all the centers of
vitality. The preacher is a student, and
as a student he must work continuously
and intently through a stated number of
hours each day. But he is more than
student; he is writer, and must write
incessantly if he is to maintain a clear
and forceful style. In addition to all this
he is a speaker, and must have such life
and grip that he can grasp a congregation and hold it to the end. In successful
public speaking the mind becomes abnor-
mally awake, every nerve is stretched to
its utmost, and an added strain is laid
upon the heart. Only a man strong in

body can bear a load so heavy through a term of years. First the stomach succumbs, then the nerves fail, then the voice grows flabby, the sword with which the preacher must do his work thus losing its edge, and his power over a congregation being hopelessly broken. This is the experience of hundreds, and other hundreds escape physical wreck only by lessening the tension and doing their work in half-hearted ways.

Let me beseech you, therefore, to take care of your body. It is difficult for any man under forty to do this; after forty we begin to be sorry for the sins of neglect in our youth. The laws of health are simple, and may be easily stated, however difficult it may be to obey them.

First of all you must have an abundance of fresh air. Men are like plants and cannot live without air. You should study in a room well ventilated, the windows being open as much as possible, and the lungs being filled now and then with

brief seasons devoted to deep breathing.
Many a man thinks himself stupid or the
book difficult to read because he is being
slowly poisoned by carbonic acid gas.
And what is good by day is good also by
night. A current of fresh air ought to
flow through your bedroom. You cannot breathe poison all night and have a
mind fresh for work in the morning.
Never cease to value the virtue of the
air of God's great out of doors. People
catch cold not because they have too
much fresh air, but because they have too
little.

Good health is largely a problem of
eating. Food is fuel, and the body like
all engines must have fuel. You are to
run your engine at high pressure and
through long distances, and therefore you
must have an abundance of fuel. Eat
abundantly. Eat all you need. Let no
rules of the books keep you from eating
as much as the body demands. I have
known more than one student to be

broken down because he did not eat enough. But do not eat too much. Most people do. Many ministers do. Over-eating is the prolific cause of innumerable diseases, and we are undoubtedly the most overfed nation on earth. To eat more than the system demands is to break down the machinery of the body, and store up trouble for years to come. Eat little in the morning, for you cannot fill the stomach with a huge breakfast and then have enough blood in your brain to do successful mental work. The students of all lands have learned by experience that to study in the morning the breakfast must be light. And this is true, even on Sunday morning, notwithstanding the hard work of the service. The meal on Saturday night should be so abundant that a light breakfast Sunday morning shall be sufficient for one's needs. Public speaking requires all the blood which the heart can supply, and if one has it in his stomach digesting his breakfast, it will not burn in his voice or throb in his words.

Take an abundance of exercise, but do not take too much. Hard brain workers require only exercise that is gentle. If you are pouring out your vitality in mental activity, you must not pour it out also in bodily exertion. There is such a thing as burning the candle at both ends, and many a man working hard with his head has supposed he must recuperate by working hard with his body, the result being complete bodily and mental exhaustion. Let your exercise be gentle and regular and as often as possible in the open air.

Along with the air and the food and the exercise you must take an abundance of rest. If you are to be hard workers, you must learn the art of recuperation. Since you are always breaking yourself down, you must learn how constantly to build yourself up. God has provided a daily rest in sleep. Take all the sleep you need. No book can tell you how much this is. It may be four hours, or six, or eight, but whatever the amount is you must take it, and he who does not take it, refuses at his peril. There are some sins which the nervous system refuses to pardon, and one of these is throwing away sleep. God has provided a weekly rest in the Sabbath. One day in seven is to be devoted to rest. It matters not what the day is, but it must be one day in seven. The Jews begin counting at one point, the Christians begin at another, the preacher must begin at still another, for on the day when his congregation is resting he must do some of his most strenuous work.

There is no commandment in the decalogue so easily forgotten as the fourth. Moses knew this and so began it with the solemn, " Remember." It is a commandment more disregarded by ministers than by any other class of believers. Many a minister does not know that the commandment is for him at all. He knows it is for others, but imagines that if he is doing good, God will forgive him for doing wrong. That is a big, black lie! Many a dear saint has been broken all to pieces by such foolish reasoning and reckless conduct. God is no respecter of persons, and every one upon whom his law falls is ground to powder.

The same sort of temptation came to Jesus. The devil told him he could jump from one of the pinnacles of the temple down into the street, and that no harm would come to him because there was a verse of scripture saying: " He shall give his angels charge concerning thee : and in their hands they shall bear thee up lest at any time thou dash thy foot against a stone." But the Son of Man could not be hoodwinked. Quick as a flash his reply was, " Thou shalt not tempt the Lord thy God." That is what ministers are doing when they do not rest one day in seven; they are tempting God. They jump from the pinnacle to the street and are bruised and broken. Many ministers do not observe any rest day at all, and those who do usually choose Monday. The reason for their choice is that they are exhausted after the work of Sunday, and being "blue" they do not attempt to work. In my opinion Saturday, not Monday, ought to be the preacher's day of rest. If he has a blue Monday, it is because there is something wrong in his way of living.

No man in fair bodily health ought to be completely exhausted by preaching two sermons on Sunday. The reason for the exhaustion is in many cases because the minister comes to his sermon with only the fag ends of his strength. He has probably postponed the writing of his sermon till Friday or Saturday. He then plunges into it with desperation and fury. He works on it all day Saturday and perhaps late Satur-

day night, and possibly into Sunday
morning. After a few hours' sleep he
goes to work again, toiling up to the
very hour for his appearance in the pulpit. He is already an exhausted man,
but in the excitement of the hour he for-
gets it. He works on his nerves. He
calls out all his reserves. The fountains
of life are well-nigh exhausted, and he
draws out of them their last drop. When
the day is over he wonders whether life
is worth living, and on the morrow he is
blue because on the verge of nervous
collapse.

A blue Monday is a danger signal
which the Lord hangs out to warn his
ministers of coming disaster. A man
should come to his pulpit fresh, with
nerves full of life and all his blood leap-
ing through his veins. He should do but
little mental work on Saturday, spending
Saturday afternoon in the open air. His
Saturday evening meal should be the best
and most elaborate meal of all the week.

The evening should be spent with his family or with friends, in a room warm with social cheer, in order that he may fall in love again with human beings. Saturday night bed-time should be the earliest of the week, and after a good night's sleep he will awake, brood over the sermon which he has prepared, and the truth will so burn in him and the tides of life will so rise and roll as to render him almost beside himself with impatience, so eager will he be to give utterance to his message. In these hurried times when congregations are likely to be made up of fagged and jaded men and women, there is special reason why the man in the pulpit should be physically recuperated and overflowingly vital.

But the weekly rest is not enough. There must be an annual rest. Every minister should have a vacation, longer or shorter, every year. It does not matter in what season, it is only important

that it should come. There is much
routine in ministerial work, and routine,
if too long continued, is ruinous to the
action of the highest powers of the
soul. There is a monotony which unless
broken leads down to the chambers of
death. A man cannot prepare two sermons, and then two more, and then two
more, and then two more, and keep on
doing that week after week, month after
month, year after year, without a break,
or a chance to get out of the treadmill and
lie down for a while in God's fields. The
land from which you expect rich harvests
must be allowed to lie fallow, and if a minister does not break the routine of sermonic work, the routine will most certainly
break him. He will become mechanical,
perfunctory, professional, and will cease
to be vital and human.

Take a vacation every year. If your
people do not consent, take it anyhow.
No minister is called upon to sacrifice his
usefulness because of the demands of

ignorant and unreasonable people. If
they remind you that the devil never
takes a vacation, say to them that that
is the very reason you are bound to take
one, since you are not following the devil,
but the prince of preachers who was
wont to say to those who labored for him,
" Come apart and rest awhile."

2. *The Mental Man.* No matter how
fine the physique, something besides body
is essential for the production of sermons.
There is a mental man inside the physical
man whose assistance is indispensable, and
whose health and growth must be carefully safeguarded. A minister must give
constant attention to the making of his
mind. Its muscles must be developed; its
nerves must be kept full of blood. The
preacher is a teacher, and how can a
teacher teach unless he knows, and how
can he know unless he uses all his faculties
of acquisition and retention? His memory
must be finely disciplined. Without it he
is pouring wine into a sieve. His imagina-

tion must be alive.   He must see in order
that he may paint.   The power of organ-
izing thought must be built up and disciplined, for it is his business to weld the
links of argument and appeal into a chain
which shall be strong enough to bind
men's hearts and minds around the cross
of Christ.

There are two kinds of preachers, — men
of thoughts and men of thought.   The
man of thoughts keeps all sorts of books
of illustrations, and drawers filled with
clippings, and envelopes stuffed with
bright ideas, and when the time comes for
the making of the sermon, he brings out
of his treasury things new and old, placing
the thoughts in a certain sequence, like so
many glass beads on a string, the string
being divided into sections by an occasional big blue bead, this bead being an
illustration.   Such a man brings his beads
before the congregation, counts them over,
spends thirty minutes in doing it, and the
people go home thinking they have been

listening to a sermon. But in a deep sense that performance is not a sermon at all. Reciting a string of thoughts is not, strictly speaking, preaching.

Preaching is the unfolding of truth; it is the evolution of an idea. One idea is sufficient to make a powerful sermon. A man who can take a great idea and by sheer force of brain unfold it until it glows and hangs glorious before the eyes of men, and so burns that hard hearts melt and consciences awake and begin to tremble, is a preacher indeed, and actually performs the work of the Lord. But the little dabbler in other men's thoughts, who fills up his time with second-hand anecdotes and stale stories, and tales intended to make people cry, never gets down to the place where the soul lives, and does not know either the preacher's agony or his reward. A congregation knows when it is in the hands of a man who is a thinker; and it also knows when it is listening to a man who is a retailer of other men's ideas.

A sermon is a rose. The text is the bud, and the preacher, breathing on the bud, causes the folded petals to open on the air and fill with fragrance the place where the saints of God are sitting. Go to the bee, young preacher; consider her ways and be wise. Where does the bee get her honey? You say out of the flowers. You are mistaken. There is no honey in the flowers. You cannot get an ounce of honey out of a hundred fields of flowers. Open a flower and there is no honey in it; only a little sweetened water. But the bee takes the sweetened water, squeezes into it a drop of her own secretion, makes to it a personal contribution, and lo! the sweetened water becomes honey. The bee did it by personal work. And so must you. All the flowers of speech and the illustrations and the anecdotes and the stories are so many posies containing nothing but a little sweetened water. You cannot feed an audience of adults on water even though it is sweetened. You can feed men only on thought, and you must do the thinking. To whatever you find you must make your own individual and personal contribution. It is only as you put your own heart and brain into your sermons that they become sweet as honey and the honeycomb.

Go to the spider, young preacher, and get from it a lesson in preaching. The spider does not weave its web out of material which is gathered from the field or the house, but the web is spun out of the substance of the spider itself. That delicate and artistic creation, the spider's web, is too fine to be made of the rough stuff of the streets. Those gossamer threads are woven out of the stuff of which the spider is made, and its miracle becomes possible only by the forthgiving of the spider's own life. If you would catch and hold the hearts of men, you must weave your sermons out of the very substance of your soul. It is not the material which other

men have gathered and organized, but the
stuff of your own spiritual self which is
demanded by the people who think. Your
personal contribution is everything. You
must pour into your sermon your own
heart's blood. Let me give you a new
definition of sermons; they are drops of
blood shed by the servants of the Lord for
the redemption of the world. More will
be said of the mental man when we come
to consider the growing of sermons.

3. *The Spiritual Man.* Man is an animal, but an animal cannot preach. He
is an intellectual being, but an intellectual
being cannot preach. He is a being created in the image of God, and endowed
with the divine spirit. Without the spirit
of God, no man, no matter what his physical prowess or his intellectual ability, can
successfully proclaim the good news of
God in Christ. It is easy to forget this.
Many men do forget it. They cannot
understand either themselves or others
because they drop out the fact that with-

out the Holy Spirit no man can speak successfully for God. A man may say: " I
have a diploma. I completed the course
of study. I was one of the best men in
my class. But no one wants to hear me
preach! Why is this?" You have left
out the one thing indispensable, — the Holy
Spirit. It is not uncommon for unsuccess-
ful preachers to compare themselves with
their successful brethren, and try to ascer-
tain why some succeed and others fail.
Their comparisons are pathetic to the
verge of tragedy. They compare their
own ideas, their figures, and their language
with those adopted by successful men, and
falling behind no whit, as they think, in
all these points, they feel the world has
much abused them, and that if the public
were not so stupid and so blind, they would
all find themselves in pulpit thrones.

O foolish men, do you not know that it is
not by rhetorical might, neither by scholas-
tic power, but by the spirit of the Lord
that a preacher preaches? It is surprising

how little depends on structure and orna-
ment and how much depends on the spirit.
Peter's sermon on the day of Pentecost
seems meager and tame enough, but then
it was impossible for Luke to report that
sermon, for he could not report the spirit
of God. The sermons of Spurgeon sound
cold and commonplace as we read them in
his volumes, and the sermons of Beecher
seem repetitious and prolix. But it is impossible to print a sermon. The most
fully reported sermon is nothing but a
skeleton. The life of the sermon lies in
the tones and accents, in the subtle fire
that burns in the syllables, and the spiritual heat which radiates from the man himself. A sermon is a man, and you cannot
print a man.

It is commonplace to say that a
preacher must have the Holy Spirit, but
it is a commonplace which every preacher
will do well to ponder. By Holy Spirit is
meant not some indefinable and mysterious essence, but the spirit that belongs to

a whole-hearted, full-statured man. The preacher must be sincere. This is cardinal. Without sincerity he is a clanging cymbal. He must not put on. Pretense is abominable. A sham tone is nauseating. Every tone should be natural and honest. The man who talks in one tone in the street and in another tone in the pulpit is a man who needs to mend his ways. Nor should he put on robes of gorgeous language, speaking in a style which is not his own. If he has read fine literature until an elegant and superb style is spontaneous and habitual, let him use it; but let him not put on a splendid diction which does not fit the form and habit of his mind. A rhetorical drum-major is not a man to lead reverent souls into the presence of the eternal. Nor should he put on energy and passion when his thought calls for neither. Why make thunder tones over an idea which is puny?

A speaker, to be effective, must be sincere. He must also be cheerful. The

Gospel is good news. The New Testament opens with a burst of music and closes with another. The Master, in the shadow of the cross, said, "Be of good cheer," and to the hard-pressed Christians of the first century St. James's exhortation was, "Count it all joy, brethren, when ye fall into divers trials." Paul, even in a Roman prison, could write, "Rejoice, again I say, rejoice." The New Testament narrates the most tragic story known to history, but is at the same time the most jubilant book in all the world. The minister who has a glum face and a doleful spirit is a man from whom the Holy Spirit has departed. He must also be a man of hope. The golden age must lie before him.

The Hebrew prophets were unlike in much, but in seeing bright things coming they were all agreed. No matter how dark and dismal was the picture which they painted of the world in which they lived, they never laid down their brush till they had tinged the horizon with golden fire. No man has a right to call attention to the terrible and tragic features of his time unless he at the same time points to the deepening splendor of a great glory bursting in the East. Sometime, somewhere, the prophets said, the city of the Lord shall be established, and its glory shall go forth into all the earth. It is significant that St. Paul calls hope the helmet of the armor which a Christian man is bound to wear. Unless a man can hold his head up, he cannot work and he cannot fight. Unless a preacher can hold up his head, he cannot preach the Gospel in tones which smite and conquer. Being a man of hope, the preacher will be a man of courage. Where is heroism more needed than in the Christian ministry?

No man should put his hand to the plow unless he is determined not to look back, no matter what his hardships be. There are obstacles and disappointments all the way. It is hard to get an education, but it is no harder for theological students than for others. It is hard sometimes to find a place in which to work, but so also it is hard for lawyers and doctors and editors to get a start. It is hard to secure a salary at all in keeping with one's deserts, but many a young man fitting himself for a business career is to-day down at the bottom, working for four or five dollars a week. It is hard not to be appreciated, and few ministers get credit for being as able men as they are. The very frequency of their appearance before the people takes away the charm of novelty and the possibility of originality, and makes even industrious and able men seem ordinary and commonplace. But preachers are not the only unappreciated men in this world. It is hard to be ignored, and it is hard to be gossiped about and misunderstood, but this has been the fate of every man who has helped make the world a better place in which to live.

It is hard — yes, it is hard, and the man who wants something easy is not called to preach the Gospel. A coward cannot read the scriptures in a tone which will fire the hearts of men, and a preacher with a whine in his soul is a preacher whose usefulness is gone. Men who are everlastingly whimpering because of their misfortunes and trials can never lift men into the joy of the Gospel; for, if one is to keep his people on the sunny side of the street, he must walk on the sunny side of the street himself. When Jesus called twelve men to preach his Gospel, he did not promise them easy times. He told them they would be like so many sheep in the midst of wolves, and though obliged to face hatred, suffering, and death, they were not to be disconcerted or afraid. He dipped his brush in "hues of midnight and eclipse," and painted dangers, sufferings, and fire-eyed opposition; but his apostles, looking on it all, never winced or faltered, and went bravely forward to do the work appointed for them to do. To read the tenth chapter of St. Matthew's gospel gives one an exalted notion of the kind of stuff out of which these twelve men were made. No wonder they turned the world upside down! They were to face the deadliest perils, and they were also to endure. In their patience they were to save their souls.

Patience is endurance. The successful minister has mastered the secret of enduring. When William Pitt was asked the quality most needed in a man fit to be prime minister of England, his reply was, "Patience." When asked what quality stood second, his reply was, "Patience." When pressed to tell what requisite was next, his reply still was, "Patience." All ministers need patience, whether ministers of an earthly sovereign or servants of the Heavenly King. One cannot work successfully with men in enterprises that are critical and vast unless he has the grace of holding on. No delay should daunt him and no disappointment should break him down. After every defeat he should rise again, and from every slough he should emerge with a face radiant with the expectation of victory.

One of the besetting sins of our age is impatience. We move more rapidly than any generation before us, and our ambition is to move faster still. In the world of mechanics and machinery, we can do everything more expeditiously than our fathers could. We can travel faster by rail and sail faster on the sea. We can make money faster, and also lose it faster, than any of our predecessors. We can manufacture goods faster and put up buildings with a rapidity worthy of the magicians of the olden tales; and, because we can do many things so swiftly, we are impatient that we cannot with equal dash do everything that we want to do. But alas! the processes of growth cannot be hastened, and when it comes to growing crops in the field or raising harvests in the mind, we are bound by the same old tedious laws by which the world was bound a thousand years ago.   Wheat grows no more rapidly now than in the days of Herodotus, and the Indian corn requires no fewer days to ripen than it did when the Indians and our fathers lived side by side on this New England soil.   Boys need the appointed years to grow to manhood and girls to grow to womanhood, and a soul can be converted or sanctified no more swiftly now than in the days when Christianity was young.   No man becomes a saint in a day or a night, and sermons, however true and God-inspired, bring forth harvests only at the end of many days.

It is important, therefore, that the young minister should have patience, that he should school himself to it, and should pray unceasingly that more and more he may become willing to wait upon the

Lord. If he allows himself to become feverish and fussy, this ungodly disposition will show itself in all his pulpit work. The servant of the Lord should have a calm eye and an untroubled heart if he is to do successfully the great work of the King. It is the man with high ideals and strenuous spirit who is most likely to become soonest disgusted with the sluggishness of the average parish; and unless he holds himself in check, he will not only infuse into his sermons a heated and a captious spirit, but he will write out his resignation before his work is well begun.

One of the curses of the modern church is the shortness of the average pastorate. Our ministers are degenerating into a band of nomads, and they wander from place to place in search of pastures which are green. Not only do the preachers lose, but the whole church of God suffers. A man cannot test himself and show what is really in him unless he has been in a church for several years, and the best and most lasting work is never done until sufficient time has elapsed for the people to know the pastor and the pastor to know the people. It requires years for the heart-doors to be opened, and it is only after they are open that the word of God runs and is glorified.

I wish that every young man might make up his mind to stay with his first church at least five years unless circumstances extraordinary render so long a stay impracticable, and that after the first term of service no pastorate of less than ten years' duration might be counted worthy of a minister or a church. It is as the years increase that a minister's influence spreads and deepens in ways which are amazing. Only after the patient laying of deep foundations is it possible for the man of God to know what sort of structure it is possible for him to build. The man who flits from place to place is almost sure to give but surface truths, and whatever impression he may make is quickly washed away; whereas, the man who stays in one field year after year draws from a well that is deep and that grows constantly deeper, and it is from the deep wells of the minister's heart that the best and most refreshing sermons flow. One of the greatest pulpit princes of recent times is Alexander Maclaren of Manchester. At the celebration of the thirty-eighth anniversary of his pastorate, he uttered these significant words, "I am quite sure that a man's influence increases in geometric ratio with the length of his pastorate." He would never have found that out had he not been a man of patience.

These then are the three men by whose combined effort you are to preach. The physical man must be strong: the mental man must be alert: the spiritual man must be true. It is the man rather than the sermon which makes the impression, and no matter what you say, you may be impotent in your work if the man behind the sermon is thin or vain or insincere. There is a warning in the words of Emerson, "What you are speaks so loud I cannot hear what you say."

III

The Growing of Sermons

THE usual expression is "making" a sermon, or "getting up" a sermon, but the "growing" of a sermon is preferable. For in a very true sense you can no more "make" a sermon than you can "make" an ear of corn, and you can no more "get up" a sermon than you can "get up" a lily of the valley. A sermon in the highest sense is a growth rather than a manufactured product, an organism and not a thing that is made. You may make something and call it a sermon—a verbal thing thirty minutes long, but a verbal creation is not necessarily a sermon even though you give it that name.

A pulpit discourse may be manufactured just as a piece of furniture. A man who makes a table picks out his pieces of wood, saws them, planes them, puts them together, and the article thus constructed is sandpapered, painted, and varnished. In the same mechanical manner it is possible to work in the study. A minister may bring out his materials, put in a piece of exegesis, add a piece of doctrine, tack on a piece of illustration, and then a piece of exhortation, and these having been nicely fitted together, he may sandpaper them and varnish them, and the whole thing polished and labeled may be carried before a congregation and called a sermon, but a sermon in reality it is not. It is too wooden. It is dead, and a sermon is always alive. A sermon grows as an apple grows, and what it needs is sun and time. You may pick it green if you are in a hurry, and if you do, it will set your people's teeth on edge. You may pick it half ripe and lose something of the flavor, or you may wait till it becomes mellow, rich, and juicy, and then the saints are glad.

A genuine sermon is an organism, a living thing with all its parts organically connected, and when you throw it out upon a congregation, it becomes a living creature with hands and feet, and immediately goes to work and takes hold of men, lifting them out of despondencies and dungeons and setting them to travel along ways that are new. It will be well for us to consider the conditions under which sermons best grow.

If a man is to produce good sermons straight onward through the years, he must be the most indefatigable of all toilers. The cardinal virtue of a prophet of God is industry. Many men do not know what work is. Some of them think they know, but they are mistaken. Many a man imagines he is working hard when in fact he is a dawdler and a shirk. Some men seem busier than they are, and not a few would rather do anything else than think.

Men are naturally intellectually lazy. This is true of all men and not at all pecul-

iar to the clergy. The average human
being wherever he is found shrinks from
any task wh' ʜ requires close and continuous attent' ɪ, and which lays a tax upon the
mind. ɪt is not because ministers are
lazier than other men that I dwell upon
the . indolence, but because laziness is
ɪ ore disastrous in their case than in any
other. Their sin finds them out and their
shame is shouted from the housetops.
The work of growing sermons requires a
more strenuous forthputting of more different faculties of the mind than is necessary in any other calling, and if one is not
capable of sustained intellectual effort and
not willing to exert his mind in season and
out of season, let him never think himself
called by God to preach.

If the clergyman has in his system any
germs of mental sloth, let him watch and
pray, for no other man in all the town
has better opportunities to take life easy.
Most men go to work under bosses who
hold their watch in their hand. The work-

man who does not appear promptly on time is reprimanded and docked. The minister works under one who also holds a watch in his hand, but both watch and overseer are invisible, and therefore are readily forgotten. A man who will take advantage of his people simply because the door is shut and he cannot be seen is a deep-dyed scamp, even if he has been ordained and writes Reverend in front of his name. But a minister can be intellectually lazy and still be so busied with parochial affairs as to feel he is earning his salary, and not realize how lazy he is.

The head of a church can do chores and run errands, and talk with good people in the streets and in their homes, and spend a deal of time inspecting the wheels and mending the belts of the ecclesiastical machinery, but all this requires little mental effort, and that is why many men prefer to do it. If a man is to be a preacher, he cannot fill up his days with the odds and ends of church administration, but must set himself down to do some honest and straightforward thinking.

Some men are tempted to be lazy because intellectually their people are so common. Their congregation reads little and thinks less, and the minister, knowing this, has no incentive to put thought into his sermons, and feels that any exposition, however faulty, or any exhortation, however feeble, will be as acceptable as the most carefully wrought-out production. But no matter what his temptations, a prophet of the Lord cannot be lazy without forfeiting his power. Unless you work as hard as Italians do when they are digging ditches, and as hod-carriers do when they are carrying mortar, and as farmers do when they are in the harvest field, and as doctors do in attending to their patients, and as merchants do in bearing the heavy burdens of financial responsibility, and as mothers do in the ordering of their households and in the rearing of their children, you have no right to stand in the pulpit on the Lord's day and as a representative of Christ tell his people how they ought to live. Learn to live first yourself.

1. Work by the watch, not necessarily with the watch ever open before you, but with a sense of time deeply grounded in your mind. Thousands of your fellow-countrymen are out of bed every morning at four o'clock. They must be in order that they may live. Tens of thousands are out of bed at five, hundreds of thousands are up at six, and millions are at their work in factory and mill at seven, having breakfasted and traveled long distances in steam or trolley cars in order to get to work on time. Shame on you if you habitually lie in bed till seven or eight or nine as your sluggish body dictates, and then arise to spend an hour on the daily papers and dawdle over a magazine, getting down to honest work it may be at ten or eleven, and possibly

not at all. A man with so little conscience ought to be whipped out of the ministry. Anthony Trollope, the English novelist, always worked with his watch before him, doing a prescribed amount of work each day, saying that as a writer he was bound by the same rules of industry as those which the other laborers of England were bound to obey. A minister of the Gospel ought not to be less conscientious than a writer of fiction.

2. Work if you can without a break. You cannot do it every day, but do it when you can. Desultory thinking, and thinking done in fits and starts between the interruptions of intruding visitors and duties, is not the kind of thinking which builds up the preacher's mind. It is good for him every day to be for a while alone. And a minister can be alone if he shuts himself in, and refuses to be disturbed. Some ministers do not believe this, but it is because they have never resolutely tried it. People are beautifully sensible

and reasonable in all such matters if a minister will take them into his confidence. If he tells them that he desires certain hours each day for uninterrupted study and then proves on the succeeding Sundays that he has really studied and not done something else, they will not only be glad to let him have his mornings, but they will be proud that they have a minister who can preach. Nothing is so galling to a congregation as the necessity of saying, "Our minister is a good man but — he cannot preach!" It may be, of course, that some crank in the parish will raise an outcry if the minister does not see him at any hour when he may choose to call, but let no one be thereby disconcerted, for the cranks, no doubt, are stationed by the predestination of Almighty God in every parish to test the patience and develop the courage of those who preach the word.

It is said that Spurgeon, when he was told that an importunate visitor insisted

on seeing him on the ground that he
was a servant of the Lord, sent back
this all-sufficing answer, " Tell the servant of the Lord that I am engaged with
his Master." The great business men of
New York City do not see every stranger
or visitor who may choose to call. They
barricade themselves behind clerks and
attendants, seeing only those who by ap-
pointment have a legitimate claim upon
their time. If men engaged in earthly
enterprises thus carefully safeguard their
strength in order to do better work, the
minister intrusted with business of the
King will not be held guiltless if he sur-
renders himself to the whims and exac-
tions of every careless passer-by.

3. Never forget you are working
for the immortal sons of God. For them
you can never afford to do work that is
slipshod. If you scamp your work for
men, you show scant reverence for their
Maker. No matter how plain and humble your congregation, you are under

obligation to do your best. You must never come down to people, but in every case go up. Ministers of the Gospel are not sent to look down on their brethren, but to be their servant and their friend. St. Paul wrote his letters to little groups of very humble folk. The churches of his day were made up for the most part of obscure laboring people, many of them being servants, with here and there a slave. The church in Corinth was not different from the churches in other places. Paul reminds the Corinthian Christians that not many wise, not many mighty, not many noble, were called. That is, there were few scholars or men of influence or representatives of high society in the Corinthian congregation. Nevertheless, in the writing of his letter Paul did his best. He wrote them one of the greatest epistles ever penned by the hand of man. In that letter he wrote a hymn of love which excels in beauty everything which Plato ever wrote. And

along with the hymn of love he sent an
argument on the resurrection which out-
strips in majesty and eloquence the proud-
est page of Aristotle.

Do not be afraid of throwing away
your best efforts on the poorest and
plainest people God lets you serve. They
may be ignorant, obscure, and uninter-
esting, but probably in the world to
come your highest joy will be the memory that when these people were far
away from the Father's house, undeveloped in the virtues which make men
strong and in the graces which make
them lovely, you were kind to them and
helped them, heartening them for fresh
efforts to travel up the long and toilsome
way. To preach to these "little ones,"
as though they were indeed the brethren
of our Lord, this is an act which in God's
universe can never be forgotten, and
which is certain to bring an exceeding
great reward.

4. Work with your spirit and on your

spirit. This is best done in prayer.
Men who would preach must pray. Few
of us pray enough. The reason why we
pray but little is because praying is hard
work. It is taxing and exhausting. We
do not easily pray. Our minds are too
undisciplined and our hearts too worldly
to come easily into communion with the
Eternal Spirit. To concentrate the attention on one who is invisible, and to bring
all the faculties into subjection and pros-
trate them before the throne requires a
forthputting of energy of which even the
strongest men are capable only for a
period exceeding brief. But this is work
which cannot be neglected. It is everything for a preacher to be attuned to
the Eternal.

The strings of human nature must be
keyed tightly if they are to give forth
music when the breath of heaven blows
through them. If sermons are to grow,
they must have sunshine. In prayer man
lets in the sun. When Martin Luther

was busiest he prayed the most; when
we are busiest we pray the least. Because
he prayed he shook the crown from the
head of the Bishop of Rome. You will
never shake the crown from the brow of
any enemy of God unless you are men
of prayer. The apostles were not mistaken when they put praying before
preaching. They were sent out to preach
the word, but they knew they could not
preach until they prayed. Their great
declaration is worthy of a place on every
minister's study wall: "We will continue
steadfastly in prayer, and in the ministry
of the word."

5. Work with your head. Use the
gray matter of the brain. Develop your
mind by bringing it into contact with the
great minds of the race. You ought to
have the best books ever written. First
of all, you must study the Bible. I do
not mean read it, but study it. It is a
hard book. Certain pages are opaque.
Many sentences are obscure. There are

apparent inconsistencies and contradictions. Many things are hard to understand. Truth lies piled up in masses, and you must organize it and put it into shape for modern uses. You must ask and seek and knock, or you will never get into the deep meanings of scripture. You must dig, and you must dig deep, and no money is better spent than on books which will help you get still deeper into this revelation which came through holy men of old.

But the Bible is not the only book. God has revealed himself through other men than the Jews. English literature contains a revelation. You ought to read poetry for vision and music and color, biography for stimulus and courage and patience, history for perspective and proportion, science for a revelation as wonderful in its way as the revelation which came through Moses and the prophets of Israel, fiction for the analysis of character and the widen-

ing of experience, and last but not least
theology, the queen of the sciences, and
all those related sciences which pay obei-
sance to the queen.   Shut yourselves up
with the great books.   Do not spend too
much time on magazines and papers.
Read the great poets and the great biog-
raphies and the great histories and the
great novels, and strive to know something of the great sciences of astronomy
and biology.   You are to read these not
in order to parade your learning before
your congregation, but because great
books make mental blood and muscle
and bone.

You ought to know ten thousand times
more than you ever say.   A preacher
influences his congregation not simply
by what he says, but by what he knows
and says nothing about.   We are not
interested in the man who tells us all
he knows.   A sermon is only a cup
of water, and it tastes better when we
know that it comes from an inexhaustible

spring. A sermon is only a drop of spray, and it has a new sparkle in it when we feel behind it the roll of the Atlantic. A preacher to preach well must have reserve power, and reserve power comes from the preacher's consciousness that he has many treasures which he need not use.

6. Work with your pen. Work a while every day. It is the pen which makes the exact man, and it is the pen which makes the accurate and forceful speaker. Writing is to many men sheer drudgery, but it is a form of drudgery which no preacher should try to escape. Nothing is so surprising to the average man as the discovery that the simplest style is, according to the testimony of all great writers, the result of enormous labor. It seems almost incredible that men should be willing to write their productions over as many times as some of the best-known writers have declared to be their practice. To write a sermon once is to some men

almost intolerable drudgery, and to write
it over three and four and five and six
times, as many pulpit princes have done,
is to the average clergyman an utter im-
possibility. With such reluctance to sub-
mit to the drudgery of the pen, no wonder
there is much slovenly and ineffective pulpit English.

An English writer of distinction was
in the habit of saying to all aspirants
for literary honors, " Fill your waste-
basket." The advice is good also for
preachers. A minister should fill his
waste-basket again and again before he
attempts to fill his people. Nothing is
more difficult to learn than the art of
using language with idiomatic grace and
force. To select the broad-shouldered
nouns and stalwart verbs which will best
carry the weight of your ideas, to choose
adjectives which will not exaggerate and
adverbs which will not give a false accent
or color, to frame the sentences with words
so clear that your truth will blaze out

through them, to whip your paragraphs into subjection to your ruling purpose so that they shall carry your thought on to fresh coronations in the hearts of those who listen to you, — that is one of the greatest achievements to which any mortal can aspire, and a victory so difficult and glorious that to win it is worth an entire lifetime of heroic and unflagging toil. Brethren, use your pen. It is the key to one of the kingdoms of power.

And now let me give you a surprising caution: Do not work too much on your sermons. You can never work too much on yourself, but to work too much on your sermons is dangerous and easy. You may work so long upon a sermon that you spoil it. It becomes too finished and has too fine a polish. It is as beautiful as a statue and as cold. It is intrusively a work of art. It smells of the lamp. It is not the spontaneous outgushing of a heart, but the dried and studied thing of a calculating brain. It is "faultily

faultless, icily regular, splendidly null.''
Avoid the perfection which smacks of
the mechanical. It is a good thing that
the sermon should be human. It may
lose nothing of its power if it have an
occasional blemish. Even to break down
in grammar or to get tied up in a sentence is not a sin which has no forgiveness.

The letters of St. Paul are all the more
interesting and endearing because they
were written hurriedly and at white heat.
He trips now and then, so eager is he
to get on, and occasionally becomes so
tangled in his construction that many a
critic has been scandalized and declared
him a bungler in the use of Greek. But
the broken phrases and the embroiled sentences all bear witness to the fact that
the apostle was in dead earnest, and after
every slip he mounts up with wings as an
eagle and lets us see what his great soul
can do.

It is an old story many times repeated, but one which never loses point, that Father Taylor, the Boston preacher to the sailors, once got so entangled in the folds of one of his rolling sentences that in sheer desperation he stopped, saying to his congregation, "Brethren, I have no idea where I started in on this sentence, and I have not the faintest conception where I am coming out, but of one thing I am absolutely certain, and that is that I am bound for the kingdom of heaven." A congregation which is sure that the preacher is bound for the kingdom of heaven and desires to take every one else with him, will not view him with a critic's eye, even though he occasionally drops below the elegance and precision of Demosthenes and Cicero.

It is easy also for a minister to spoil his people. He may train them to expect word pictures and thrilling pieces of denunciation and appeal. He may educate men to look upon the pulpit as a stage, and upon the preacher as an actor, and they may

come to church just as they would go to
the art gallery or the opera. It is bad
for the preacher when his parishioners
begin to prattle about his "beautiful"
sermons, and endeavor to get others to
come to church because they have such
a "beautiful" preacher. If the pound
cake is so artistically decorated that every
one begins to talk about the frosting, it
will be well to feed the people for a season on brown bread. But the most disastrous result of overworking on a sermon
is the impoverishment which may come to
a minister's own soul. He may work on
his sermons until he becomes decrepit and
palsied in intellectual power and spiritu-
ally thin. He may make so much of the
sermon as to break down his health. It
may become a sort of white elephant for
which he must carry water every day.
He may think about it so much that it
will haunt him in his sleep, and give him
no peace day or night. The minister is
on the way to physical bankruptcy when

the sermon pursues him like a fiend through the week.

And sympathy with men may also be destroyed. One may become such an artificer in thought and in language as to become fastidious and finical, caring more for the polish of a sermon than for the salvation of a soul. Many a man has worried more over a paragraph in his sermon than over a soul going down to perdition. The man who begins to idolize the sermon, and worships it every day, will sometimes become so fussy and pedantic that he cannot trust himself to say anything whatever unless it has been carefully wrought out with the pen. A man in this frame of mind is unfitted for the pulpit. The preacher must of all men be human, and a preacher is no longer human when he cannot at least sometimes open his mouth and talk out of the abundance of his heart like a man.

By working all week on a sermon,

the minister robs himself of opportunity
to range through those wider realms of
thought which are absolutely indispensable to the growing soul. I have known
men to work so hard upon their sermons
that they worked themselves down into
intellectual shallowness and pulpit impo-
tence. A sermon is nothing but a key;
it must be cast and filed, but it must not
be filed until there is no strength left in
the hand which is to turn it. The feeding of the hand is surely as important
as the filing of the key. A sermon is a
sword. It is important that the sword
should have an edge. Sufficient time
should be given to its sharpening. But
it is also important that there should be
a strong right arm capable of swinging
the sword. A sermon is a rose. You
gain nothing by picking at its petals.
Your supreme work is keeping your heart
so full of Christian blood that sermonic
roses will bloom spontaneously on your
lips. Therefore, work on your soul more

than on your sermon, more on the soil than on the thing which you wish to bring to market.

The art of preaching is something like the art of agriculture. The successful farmer works incessantly on the soil. He fertilizes it, changes the fertilizer from time to time, shifts his crops now to one field, now to another, always studying the condition of the soil. He breaks up one field, lets another field lie fallow, works with the soil in all sorts of ways that every field may be rich and mellow. The secret of good farming lies in constant working with the soil. It is, of course, important that the seed should be good, but good seed avails nothing in an exhausted soil. Now a preacher is nothing but a spiritual farmer. His mind is his farm. From that farm he must bring repeated harvests for the feeding of the sons of God. Unlike the farmer he expects a harvest every seven days. This is a tremendous drain. Every week two sermons must be garnered, and the sermons will be determined by the nature of the soil. Unless the soil is fertilized heavily from day to day, and unless it is worked with, and that unceasingly, the soil is certain to grow shallow, and in the pulpit there will be an exhausted man.

That is the reason why so many ministers cross the dead line early. They fail to work with the soil. Many of them are honest and faithful men who have tried with loyal heart to do their work in the fear of God and for the advancement of his kingdom, but they have worked too exclusively upon their sermons and have not built up their mind, and the result is that year by year they have dwindled in the pulpit, and by and by have not been able to preach acceptably at all. Many a minister is not so good a preacher at forty as he was at thirty, and hundreds cannot preach so well at fifty as they did at forty. A congregation knows at once whether or not there is in the pulpit an exhausted man. No experience or learning is a substitute for freshness and vitality. Young men who are fresh at thirty are immeasurably superior to men, thin and exhausted at fifty, for the work of preaching is the work of lifting, and lifting requires a man of strength. Men who work incessantly on the soil, building their mind up four square in mental alertness and capacity, do not cross the dead line ever, but work on successfully till the sun goes down.

The preacher is like the horticulturist, and sermons are like roses. The man who would produce fine roses must pay attention to the conditions under which fine roses grow. The soil must be rich, the sunshine must be abundant, the moisture must be sufficient, and simply by securing these conditions the roses come forth of themselves. Man supplies the conditions and God brings forth the roses. God lets man help him bring forth roses, but man's work is confined largely to the culture of the soil.

The man who flings himself enthusiastically into the production of his sermons, determined that he will give his strength and time to the processes of sermon building, is a man who will surely fail because he is beginning wrong. In the deepest sense God alone makes sermons, and what man must do is to work incessantly on the soil. The man who keeps his soul fertilized and mellow will never, when Sunday comes, find himself without a sermon.

The problem of problems then for every preacher is not how to make a sermon, but how to cultivate the soul in such a way as that there shall be sap sufficient to produce sermonic blossoms which shall make the Sabbaths fragrant, and leaves which shall be for the healing of the congregation.

Let me urge you then to set aside one morning from the very start on which you will not work upon your sermon — work on everything else than that. Put your sermon topic into your mind as early as you wish, and let it lie there undisturbed. There is such a thing as unconscious cerebration, and probably this goes on even in one's sleep. It is surprising how a subject once dropped into the mind gathers round it kindred material from the experience which comes to one from day to day. A magnet drawn through sand in which there are iron filings will not more surely pick out the iron than will an idea held in the mind pick out related ideas from every book one reads and from every conversation. An active-minded man cannot cast a text into his soul without discovering on its removal, after the lapse of several weeks, that other thoughts have crystallized around it and that a sermon is in the process of formation.

This unconscious sermonic work will go forward through the days. But on one day of every week banish your sermon from your conscious thought and give yourself to some favorite and rewarding study. For a day work only

on the soil. At first one day will probably be all that you can spare, for in the
early years a deal of time is required to
give the sermon form. Special reading
must be done, throwing light on next Sunday's subject, and the structure of the
sermon is sometimes baffling, and language
too is intractable and stubborn; and what
with his language and his plan and his
ideas, the beginning preacher has much
to do.

Four mornings on two sermons are
none too many for the average man
through the beginning years. But as soon
as possible the minister should cut down
his sermon mornings to three, giving two
entire mornings to biblical, scientific, or
historical studies. On these two mornings
let him work upon the soil, and his people
will discover that his sermons have new
fragrance and flavor. After a few years
it may be that the sermonic work can be
crowded into two mornings, and three
whole mornings be left for the building

up of mental nerve and bone. Wide study
in these days is essential that men may
see our problems in true perspective and
right relations. A little man with narrow
view can cause a world of trouble. Our
problems are intricate and difficult, and
only ministers of extensive learning are
capable of grappling with themes so
great.

The three mornings given to church history or Christian doctrine will make you
wiser when you come to deal with the
next problem that confronts you in your
parish work. They will also give you a
balance of judgment and mental poise
which your people will feel, although they
may not know their cause. It may be that
after years of training you can give shape
to two sermons in a single morning, re-
serving four mornings sacred for study
and research. It is said that Dean Farrar,
in his later years, never spent more than
three hours on a sermon, and that is probably enough for any man who is full of

the Christian spirit and has a disciplined and well-furnished mind. I suppose that in the ideal preacher's life there would be no time at all set aside for working on the sermon, but that the preacher simply doing his work from day to day, and keeping his mind moving through atmospheres impregnated with ideas, would on the Lord's day find a message already formulated in his heart, and be able to stir men's souls and lift them, simply by opening his mouth and allowing the message to come out.

But no such ideal preaching is possible without long preliminary years of patient and painstaking toil. There are men who have approached it. I think I have read somewhere that Spurgeon once declared that if he were given seven days in which to prepare a sermon, he would devote all the week but the last half hour to other things, and get his sermon within these last thirty minutes. Spurgeon was an indefatigable worker. He could do as much work in a day as ten ordinary men. He had an immense library which he knew how to use, and he was also working constantly with men. Living thus close to God and working thus enthusiastically with men, it was possible after long years of practice for him to formulate a sermon in half an hour.

Our greatest American preacher was able to do the same. Henry Ward Beecher, in his early years, worked assiduously with books and pen, but in later life he often prepared his sermon after his Sunday morning breakfast. This does not mean that he did not work all through the week. His active brain was never idle. His great heart was always engaged in some mighty labor. As he himself once expressed it, he was like a woman with a pan of dough; he was kneading the dough all the time. On Sunday morning he simply gave shape to material which had in his soul become thoroughly and vitally his own. Or to change the figure, the cream

kept rising through the week, and on the
Lord's day he skimmed the cream, and
gave it to the people.

What is a sermon but a cup of cream
skimmed from the preacher's life ? It
is said that one of the most noted
preachers of London usually prepares
his sermon on the day on which it is
to be delivered. He works incessantly
through the week, and then on Sunday
gives utterance to the truth which is at
that time uppermost in his soul. But all
such hasty preparation of the letter of
the sermon should never be attempted
until after years of stern self-discipline
and long-continued practice in the art of
self-expression. The sermon at its best
estate is not a fine oration or a labored
argument, but the simple testimony to the
reality of things spiritual and eternal of
a witness whose life is hid with Christ
in God.

Make the tree good. This is the one
thing necessary. The sermon is the man,

and upon the man everything depends. Pulpit power rests not on your learning nor on your mastery of the technique of expression, but on the radiance and sweetness of your personality. You must be so good and true and Christlike that you yourself shall seem to be a part of the Christian revelation, and the eternal truth of God seem to be bursting into fresh splendor on your lips. Any man can repeat the words of Jesus and the apostles, but not every man can repeat them as though they were indeed his native speech. Any man can toy with the conceptions of the sacred scriptures, but not every one can move among them as though they were features of the familiar world in which he lives and moves and has his being. You should be so filled with the Holy Spirit that helpful, precious pearls of speech shall fall as naturally from your lips as miracles did from the finger tips of Jesus, and you ought to live so near to God that when you speak, the place in which you stand shall be filled with holy light, and all the people going homeward shall feel a spiritual peace and exaltation, knowing that something beautiful has passed their way.

IV

Form and Manner

WHEN a man appears before us with a
message, the heart has three questions.
The first is, "Who is he?" If he is a
lunatic, then that information is sufficient.
We do not care to listen any more. If,
however, he is a man of sanity and intelligence, there is a second question, "What
is his message?" Is it a triviality or a
vagary or an explosion of prejudice or passion, sound and fury signifying nothing?
If so, no matter who he is, we do not care
to hear him. But if he is a man of sense
delivering a sober message, then there is a
third question, "How is he going to say
it?" Will he deliver his message bunglingly
and obscurely, slovenly and with an insult
to taste, or will he present it in a way which

will open the heart and make the new truth beautiful? Who is he, what is his message, how is he delivering it, — these are the three questions which every congregation is sure to ask. To the third question your attention is now invited. It is not the first question, to be sure, nor is it yet the second, and because it is only third there are those who pass it by altogether. To them the only things important are that the messenger should be reliable and that the message should be momentous, and with these things settled, it matters not what is the form or manner. The preacher who reasons thus is guilty of a cardinal blunder which will cripple him in all his life and work.

Above all the other religions of the world the Christian religion relies upon the tongue. There are religions which rely upon the sword, and there are others which rely upon the state, and there are others which rely upon the example of dumb devotees, but the Christian religion from the beginning has relied upon the tongue. The founder of Christianity was a preacher, and the men whom he sent out were ordained to preach. They were to take no weapons with them; the world was to be overcome simply by their words. The religion of Jesus of Nazareth enthrones and glorifies the tongue.

Language thus assumes a place of unique significance in the work of the Christian minister. It is the instrument by which he is to work out his purposes, the weapon by which he is to subdue the world. It is the rod by which he is to work his miracles. Demosthenes struck the Greeks and the Greeks struck the King of Macedon. Peter the Hermit struck Europe and Europe struck the Turk. Wendell Phillips struck the North and the North struck down slavery. You must with your tongue so strike your congregation that your congregation shall want to smite down every form of evil. Language is the train on which the ideas

of redemption are to be conveyed from the
preacher's soul to others. "Take heed
to your language," then, would seem to
be an exhortation to which every minister
of Christ should give ready ear.

Just as in certain cities the railroad train
stops and every wheel of every car is carefully inspected, men with flaring torches
and hammers of steel, looking with eye
and listening with ear for any open or con-
cealed defect, and all in order that not a
single life may be put in jeopardy in the
crossing of river or climbing of mountains,
so ought the words of every sermon be
subjected to the closest scrutiny that not
one thought shall fail to make the transit
from the preacher's to the hearer's soul.
For what are words but verbal cars in
which are conveyed the food and raiment
for the children of the King! In them
are packed thought and hope and love,
sympathy and tenderness and pity, uplift
and outlook and new horizon, and all
these must be carried from the soul of

the preacher into the souls of those for whom these treasures are intended.

A preacher intent on his work must give constant attention to his words. It is too often forgotten that language is the body of thought and that thought depends for its effectiveness on its body. It is with ideas as it is with men, — they are worthless upon earth without a body. No disembodied man has ever done anything in history, neither has a disembodied idea. The ideas which are mighty are the ideas which are expressed, and the ideas which prevail are those which have received the most vigorous and stalwart expression. The body of thought must be nourished just as truly as the body of man. Language must be fed if it is to be healthy, and thin and pallid language is as feeble and ineffective in the realm of thought as are anæmic and emaciated men in the realm of the world's work and battle. To feed his vocabulary and nourish his style is one of the most

important works which a preacher has
to do.

And while this is important for every
minister of Christ, whatever his ecclesiastical connections, it is doubly impera-
tive for a minister who belongs to any
branch of the Christian church which has
laid aside the sensuous symbols of mediæ-
valism.   There is something about the
celebration of the mass which is warming.
The great altar, the candles, the incense,
the robes, all appeal to the eye and shed
a radiance into the heart of the sympa-
thetic worshiper.   The paintings and the
pictured windows and the statues in
churches which have discarded the incense and the candles, all appeal to the
eye and serve to rob worship of its pale-
ness and coldness.   But in many a church
there is nothing of the dim religious light.
There are no storied windows, no glorious paintings, no statues of our Lord or
his apostles.   All is plain and drab and
bare.   Upon the minister depends the

lighting up of all the worship. He must do this work with his words. His phrases must be candles giving forth a sacred light. His sentences must be paintings picturing things which the heart adores. His paragraphs must be incense filling all the place with a heavenly aroma. His words must give to the church color and fragrance, and life and fire, and the whole sermon beautiful with scented and tinted words must leave the soul flooded with melody in the immediate presence of God. With no liturgy and no symbolism, bare and naked indeed is the worship of a Protestant church if the preacher uses only threadbare and faded words.

The power of language can scarcely be overestimated. Arnold says that Gray doubled his force by his style. So can every preacher. President Eliot of Harvard does not put the case too strongly when he says that "it is a liberal education which teaches a man to speak and write his native language strongly, ac-

curately, and persuasively. It is a sufficient reward for the whole long course
of twelve years spent in liberal study."
President Eliot owes not a little of his
wide influence over American thought to
the fact that he is master of English.
When one studies the men who are to-
day foremost in the pulpit, he discovers
that without exception they are men with
great gifts of expression. The man who
has probably exerted the widest influence
within the last ten years over the religious
thought of America could not have done
it had it not been for his style. His
language is as clear as a mountain brook,
with his thoughts like shining pebbles
at the bottom of it. For his purpose the
style is well-nigh perfect, luminous, and
transparent as the almost matchless diction
of Voltaire.

Another American preacher subdues
and solemnizes his congregation by means
of his beautiful and stately English. He
has been a student of poetry and phi-

losophy, and his style has in it something of the majesty of Milton, with now and then a hint of the massiveness of Shakespeare, and here and there the sweetness and the melody of Tennyson. The style is not so clear as that of our other preacher, but even the occasional obscurity is not without its charm. There are masses of golden haze, but it is the haze that lies on the bosom of a wide, deep sea. One of the mightiest of living English preachers has a style quite different still. His language fits his thought as tightly as the skin fits the flesh. It contains no wrinkle, and is so natural and so true that unless you sit before it as a critic and pay close attention to the words, you will not notice the language at all. Style is perfect when it becomes invisible.

Brethren, believe in the power of words. They have a force almost divine, and this force is yours if you know how to use it. Think of the great work which you must

do. By means of words you must help
men to see the sublime contours of great
duties and the shining outlines of fair
ideals. By language you are to cause the
blind to see, and also the deaf to hear.
By words you are to help men hear that
music of the spirit world which soothes
and charms and lifts and blesses. By
words you are to make men feel. You
are to control for an hour the emotional
tides of the heart. You are to compel
men to feel the smart and sting of con-
demned sinners and also the raptures of
forgiveness. You are to bring men to
decision, helping them to choose, and their
choice though brief is yet endless. Since
all this and more must be done by means
of words, how foolish for any minister to
neglect the study of expression. Whatever gift a man may have at the beginning,
it should be cultivated through the years,
and every year should be regretted which
does not witness a progress in the mastering of words.

The human heart is sensitive to simple and lovely speech. The amœba, one of the lowest of microscopic organisms, is not insensible to color. It has no eyes, but in some mysterious way it feels a difference in colors. There is no congregation, however untrained and undeveloped, which cannot feel the difference between purple and dull-colored speech. The plainest and least-cultivated people will respond to words fitly spoken, and the dullest listener will be aroused by a paragraph which gives forth a flash of crimson or a gleam of gold. You must be a man of visions and you must be also a man of words, and the work of fitting them together is one of the most critical and delicate tasks which a prophet of the Lord is called upon to do. The best English spoken anywhere ought to be heard in the Christian pulpit.

Endeavor to avoid mispronunciations. Many ministers are inexcusably careless on this point. There are men who go on mispronouncing familiar words for years, and it seems as though the mispronounced words are the very words which most frequently occur. There are in almost every congregation cultured people to whose ears a mispronunciation is a blow, and a person of taste cannot be struck again and again on the same nerve without the nerve crying out in pain. Use the dictionary and use it often. Keep it out beside your Bible. Whenever in doubt consult it. Go to it even though you are well-nigh certain that you already know. Let every unfamiliar word lead you to it, and get out of bed if need be to settle a dictionary problem which has risen in your mind. There are young people in every congregation to whom a mispronunciation is an unpardonable offense. Verbal blunders prove to them that the preacher is at least on one point ignorant, and being ignorant on one point he may be ignorant on all. It is possible to weaken one's influence forever by slips which might easily have been avoided.

And then beware of worn-out words. A minister's vocabulary is subjected to terrific usage, and it will grow old and threadbare unless constantly renewed. Unless he is alert he will find himself using the same word again and again until it becomes odious or a joke. When a preacher uses the same word twenty times in his prayer, and then begins to use it twenty times or more in his sermon, the mind is distracted from the thought, and the hearer begins to calculate how soon the word will come out again.

It is well from time to time to cull out the poor abused and broken-down words and shut them up in an asylum until they recover from their exhaustion. Words have nervous prostration, as human beings have, and when long overworked they should have an outing and a rest. Avoid the use of any dialect unknown to the people to whom you preach. There are various dialects used by Americans, and the preacher is likely to have his own. The lawyers have a dialect and the doctors have a different one, and the theologians one different still. Avoid the dialect of every special class, and use the broad, plain, human speech of God's common people. When our missionaries go across the sea, they give years to mastering the language of the people to whom they have been sent. The time is well spent, for no pentecost is possible until men hear the gospel in the language in which they were born.

There are three rules which should never be forgotten. First of all be clear. You must be clear. If you are not clear, how can you be understood, and what is the use of preaching if people do not understand what you say? St. Paul has expressed the opinion of every man of sense upon this matter: "I had rather speak five words that I might teach others than ten thousand words in an unknown tongue." All the great preachers from Paul to Moody have agreed upon that one point. Augustine was a teacher of grammar and rhetoric, and had a fondness for the rotundity and finish of florid Latin, but when he became a preacher, he laid aside his polished rhetoric and spoke in the Latin of the common people. Martin Luther always kept his eye upon the peasants, saying that if he could speak in language which they could understand, then all classes would be instructed and edified.

Make it your ambition to be clear. It is your business to be understood. If you are not intelligible to every attentive listener of average intelligence, then offer no excuses, but find out what the trouble is. Do not say you are too deep, for the chances are you are knee deep in the mud. Deepest water is always clear, and it is when we reach a puddle that we cannot see the bottom. Your lack of clearness is in all probability due to shallowness, and by becoming deeper you will be more easily understood. Do not think you are great just because you can preach only to culti-vated people. That is the sign of a

mediocre preacher. The great preachers
through the centuries have all been able to
reach all classes of the people. Great
poets do the same. The poems of Homer
were appreciated both by Pericles and also
by the sausage sellers in the streets of
Athens. The poems of Virgil were relished
by the Emperor Augustus and also by the
shepherds and vine-dressers of Italy. The
poems of Shakespeare were the delight of
the greatest wits of the Elizabethan court,
and were also popular among the ground-
lings from the lowest streets of London.
Robert Burns warms the hearts of the
greatest Scottish theologians, and stirs the
blood of the farmer boy following the plow.

It is characteristic of greatness that
it appeals to the universal human heart.
America's two greatest preachers, — and
the only two supremely great, — Henry
Ward Beecher and Phillips Brooks, could
preach to students and professors and
also to artisans and servant girls. If
you cannot be understood except by the

elite, it is not because you are so deep, but because your organ is deficient in the number of its stops. The deepest preacher of the ages was Jesus of Nazareth, and all his language is simplicity itself. What is simpler than this? "He that would save his life must lose it," but it is deeper than plummet can sound. What is more easily understood than this? " Except ye become as a little child ye cannot enter into the kingdom of God," but who can fathom the depths of it? The man who lay on Jesus' breast was also simple in his style. The first chapter of the fourth gospel is written for the most part in monosyllables, but it is the deepest page of composition ever written. It was Paul who said so simply, " Christ died for our sins," but even the angels try to see the bottom of it and are not able. If, therefore, a preacher deals in long and opaque words, it is not because his thought is deep, but because he has not yet mastered the art of putting things.

Another rule is: Be simple. The exhortation of Charles Lamb to Coleridge, "Cultivate simplicity," should be heeded by the preacher. Elaborateness is out of place in these hurried days, and rhetorical tucks and flounces should be mercilessly cut off. Milton said that poetry should be simple, sensuous, and impassioned, and that is also what a sermon ought to be. It should be simple in its language, vivid in its imagery, and shot through and through with subtle fire. Daniel Webster still holds his place as one of America's greatest orators, and one of the secrets of his power is the simplicity of his style. While yet a young man he came to the conclusion that, as he was to earn his living by talking to plain people, it was necessary that he should learn to use plain language. In simplicity of diction Webster has never had but one superior, and that is Abraham Lincoln. Lincoln's speech at Gettysburg registers the high-water mark of effective English prose, and that speech is the simplest in our literature.

But how can one be simple? By the study of the masters. Be a constant reader of great books. Read Newman for music, and Ruskin for color, and Carlyle for pictures, and John Morley for discrimination, and Mark Rutherford for simplicity. Read Tennyson as long as you live. His "Idylls of the King" are in my judgment the finest piece of English written in the nineteenth century. Of course you will all read Shakespeare, the unrivaled master of human speech. Read him for his simplicity and also for the art of using short and vivid words. Contrast the English of the speech he puts into the mouth of Mark Antony with the English of many modern sermons.

"I am no orator, as Brutus is;
    But, as you know me all, a plain blunt man,
    That love my friend; and that they know full well
    That gave me public leave to speak of him:
    For I have neither wit, nor words, nor worth"—

Mark those monosyllables. Would we have used them? No. We would have

said, "For I have neither mental acumen,
nor an extensive vocabulary, nor ethical
significance."   That is what is the matter
with much of our modern preaching; it is
too full of "ethical significance" and "extensive vocabulary" and "mental acumen,"
and has not enough of this "wit and words
and worth."

> "Action, nor utterance, nor the power of speech,
>   To stir men's blood!"

Mark that!   We would have said "arouse
men's emotions," but Shakespeare knows
how to find the heart, and his words jab
like rapiers — "stir men's blood!"

> "I only speak right on;
> I tell you that which you yourselves do know;
> Shew you sweet Cæsar's wounds, poor, poor dumb
>   mouths."

Do you notice that pathos?   Change those
monosyllables into "miserable, pitiable,
inarticulate mouths," and all the pathos
has vanished.

> "But were I Brutus,
> And Brutus Antony, there were an Antony

Would ruffle up your spirits, and put a tongue
In every wound of Cæsar, that should move
The stones of Rome to rise and mutiny."

That is the kind of English which preachers need, and the more you have of it the mightier you will be in swaying the hearts of men. The list would not be complete without the Bible. It is Shakespeare and Tennyson, Ruskin and Carlyle, Newman and Mark Rutherford combined. You will never preach as God intended you to preach unless you are a constant, keen-eyed student of the language of the scriptures.

But language to do its full and perfect work must have the interpreting voice. No matter what the preacher's mental gifts or written style may be, if he lacks the flexible and expressive voice, he goes maimed and halting to his work. The voice is the most subtle and mysterious of all the organs of the soul. It seems to be halfway between the body and the spirit, and to be the product and also the

servant of them both. The voice of
the preacher should be clear and flexible,
taking color easily and making mental
and emotional valuations with rapidity
and precision. Many a preacher does
not exert upon his congregation more
than a fraction of his power, because he
stands behind a stiff and unsympathizing
voice. If the man's words say one thing
and his voice says another, if with his language he appeals and with his tones he
repels, he is working at cross purposes,
and much of his energy is thrown away.
If the sermon is a heart-to-heart talk of
the preacher with his people, then it is
desirable that his heart should throb
and pulsate in his tones. Vocal culture,
therefore, is an art which no student
for the ministry should thoughtlessly
pass by.

But vocal culture, however important,
has long been in disrepute. Elocution is
considered even by many intelligent and
well-informed people as something me-

chanical and superficial, a sort of pastime
for young ladies, but nothing serious
enough to deserve a place in the curriculum of earnest-hearted men. This
prejudice has held sway in many of our
seminaries, the result being that the
teacher of elocution has been usually
the poorest-paid member of the faculty,
or has been merely a visiting instructor
with no official standing whatever. And
there is a reason for all this. Too often
the teachers of elocution have been shallow and uneducated men, teaching in a
mechanical way, and running their pupils
into a common mold, so that all the members of the same school have come out
with similar tones and gestures, every
pupil thus being spoiled. Moreover, a
little knowledge is a dangerous thing,
and in no department of human learning
is this so true as in the science and art
of elocution. A little elocution is indeed
ridiculous. A man who studies voice and
gesture just long enough to be conscious

of them cuts a sorry figure when he comes before the people.

Elocution is a curse unless studied so long and patiently that all its scaffolding disappears, and there is left no trace of the various processes by which the voice has been redeemed. But voice culture in itself is one of the noblest and finest of the arts, and there is no reason why men should not learn how to speak as well as women learn how to sing. One does not speak well naturally any more than one sings well by nature, and unless a minister studies the art of tone production, he is almost certain to suffer for his neglect. The teacher of elocution should be one of the ablest of men, and his salary should be not a whit less than the highest.

It takes a great man to be a safe teacher of the voice. He must know not only the voice, but the body and also the mind and also the heart. In voice production the whole being, body, soul, and spirit, is implicated, and the teacher who would instruct men in the art of speaking must know human nature through the entire gamut of its capacities and powers. His chief work is that of liberation. He must set the captive free. It is often said that preachers should speak naturally; but ah, there's the rub! Not one man in ten speaks naturally unless he has been trained. Men are all bound round and tied up with bad habits, and the teacher of elocution must untie the knots. The mental excitement caused by appearing before an audience leads men to do all sorts of curious and unnatural things with the muscles of the arms and throat, and simply to be himself a man needs a competent instructor.

Indeed, that is about all the voice teacher has to do. It is not for him to dictate to his students where they shall place their emphasis or when they shall make their gestures. His work is to set all the muscles free that the soul may be at liberty to do unimpeded what it will. The hand must be set free so that the fingers shall not be tied, and the arms must be freed that gestures may not proceed from the elbow, and the lower jaw must be liberated that the tones may not be squeezed, and the constrictions must all be taken from the throat that the voice may not be cramped, and the muscles of the back must be relaxed that the tones may not lack sweetness, volume, and depth, and all the muscles of the chest must be trained that the tones may not be breathy; in short, there is scarcely a muscle in the body which may not help or mar the voice, and the teacher of vocal culture, stripping off all these fetters, says to the prisoner, "Come forth." An elocution teacher who understands his business is one of the best friends a student of theology can have.

That there is not in every theological séminary of America a competent and well-paid professor of voice culture is a scandal for which we ought to hang our heads in shame. When one thinks of the hundreds of preachers who are all the time troubled with their throats, and of the scores who break down altogether, and of the long-suffering congregations listening to uncultivated voices of men upon whose tongue the Gospel becomes a nasal or a rasping thing, irritating where it ought to soothe, and wounding where it ought to heal, one feels like hurling thunderbolts of wrath against the system of theological training by which this awful tragedy is made possible to this present hour.

A few words of counsel are all that can be given : —

1. Never put on a tone. Let every tone be sincere. Every affectation in the pulpit subtracts from the preacher's power. If you use an oily tone, or a sanctimonious tone, or a whining tone, or a graveyard tone, you are making yourself unnatural and closing the hearts of your hearers against you.

2. Avoid the devil of monotony. Its name is legion. There is a monotony of rate and one of pitch and one of emphasis and one of force and one of accent and one of cadence, and not one of the unhallowed brood will come out even by prayer and fasting. Nothing but a teacher will answer in dealing with diseases of the voice. The reason is that for the voice there is no looking-glass, and no man can safely trust his ear. The most terrible and patent defects will escape the keenest man alive until they are pointed out by an acute-eared teacher.

3. Do not overdo. Delsarte never said a brighter thing than this, "Mediocrity is not the too little, but the too much." It is one of those profound sayings which become the better appreciated the longer they are pondered. All second-rate singers overdo. They make too great an effort. They squirm and twist and make wry faces, and give the impression that singing is a tremendous feat. Great

singers sing with consummate ease. Second and third-rate actors always overdo. They put on too much. We call them stagey and theatrical, and pass them by, while we give our attention to the star, who, if he is of the first magnitude, is so natural we feel we could act that well ourself.

Second-rate preachers always overdo. They use too many adjectives, too many gestures, too many ideas, too much force. They pound the pulpit, and this invariably pushes the people farther off. You cannot pound an idea into the human mind. An idea is a flower. You can shake its perfume on the air, but that requires no bluster. An idea is a jewel. You can twirl it before your congregation, that the light of every facet may fall upon the eye, but that requires no muscle. Even if you count an idea a projectile, which is to be fired into the substance of the soul, even then it is possible to use too much force. When they first made the great projectiles with which to sink a battleship, they tipped them with the hardest steel, and found that by the impact the projectile was shattered to pieces. It was later on discovered that by tipping them with softer metal the projectiles had greater penetrating power, and, instead of breaking into pieces, plowed deep into the plates of solid steel. If you want to get a great truth deep into the human heart, then tip it with a gentle tone.

4. Be sensible. Remember that a congregation is nothing but a man. It is not a colossus to be attacked by rhetorical bludgeons, or a baby to be tickled by vocal pyrotechnics, or a monster to be tricked and trapped by oratorical stratagems and devices. To speak to a man, you must be one yourself. Never endeavor to be eloquent. It may be that God will let you be eloquent a half dozen times in your life, but I am sure you cannot be eloquent if you try to be. And never declaim. Declamation makes a

noise and interests the children, but grown-up people care nothing for it. There is nothing more monotonous than steady declamation, unless it be continuous eloquence. And do not struggle to make an impression. If you do, you will not make the kind of impression that you want to make. And when the sermon is over, never run round and ask what sort of an impression the sermon made. Only an imbecile would be excusable for asking a question so unutterably silly. And when you go to bed, do not lie awake and worry about the impression that you made or did not make.

A man must speak his message, taking care that it be clear and true, and then leave all the impressions in the hand of God. The fact is, no preacher knows what impressions are the deepest or just when or where they are made. In walking through the woods after a storm, we hear the creaking of a broken branch, and by and by, with terrific thunder, it comes crashing down across the path. It startles us, but we do not bring it home. But on our return we discover a bur sticking to our garment. When and where we got it we do not know. We passed it, we touched it, it clung to us, it seized us without hurrah and clamor, and unknowingly we brought it home. So it is with truth. The sermons that rattle and thunder are not the sermons that stay with us longest. They startle and they excite a momentary wonder, but we do not bring them home. The truths which we are carrying with us to our eternal home are truths which we have passed near at some point or other along our earthly pilgrimage, and they, touching us, have stuck to us; and because the spirit of God is in them, they keep clinging to us and we to them, although we cannot tell just how or when or why they and we first came together. Scatter God's truths through your congregation, and rest assured that some one will carry one of them home!

5. Be yourself. You are strong only when you are yourself. You are persuasive only when you speak in your mother tongue, and of those things which you yourself do know. If you walk on the stilts of other men's high phrases, or wrap yourself in the embroidered language of men of genius long since dead, you will be as impotent as David was the day he fitted on Saul's armor. Use the pebble taken from the brook which flows by your door. Use the sling which you have used from boyhood and which belongs to you by the will of God. Let other men preach as they will, you preach as you must. True to yourself, speaking as you are led, the Gospel on your lips will have an accent which it has never had before since the world began, — an accent needed to fill out the music of the full-toned proclamation of the good news of God.

6. Be natural. This is the sum of the whole matter. Do not push the voice

into clerical cadences, but let it flow out of an open throat, breaking into syllables which tell truly what you think and feel. Do not push the language into inflated and bombastic forms, but let it flow as naturally as a brook through one of God's own green meadows. Do not shove the thought into artificial altitudes, but let it move along the level on which you do your ordinary thinking. If you are altogether natural, you will become invisible. Style is perfect when it cannot be seen. Jesus was a perfect speaker. There is no recorded criticism of his style. Men would have criticised it had they seen it, but they never saw it. They saw nothing but his thought. Some men saw it, and their souls were filled with rapture. Others saw it, and they were stung to madness and fiery indignation. Men simmered and sizzled as he spoke, muttering to themselves, talking to one another, crying out by way of approbation or condemnation. Every one boiled over, some with love, and some with hate, so mighty was his speaking. He is the model for us all. A preacher really great speaks the Gospel so simply and so truly that all the congregation, looking toward him, see no man but Jesus only.

V

The Place of Dogma in Preaching

THE phrasing of my subject seems to take it for granted that there is a place for dogma in preaching. This, I know, is rather a hazardous assumption, for there are men in large numbers, intelligent and influential and Christian, who believe that there is no place whatever for dogma in the Christian religion. Christianity, they say, is a matter of feeling, a thing of the spirit; the bond of union is sentiment, not thought, and as soon as you introduce dogma you give occasion for differences and contentions and bitterness of heart. These men carry us down the centuries and show us how generation after generation has been teased and fretted into ugliness and torn into factional shreds by the everlasting disputation concerning dogma, and turning their back upon it, they shun it as the black beast of Christian history. These, of course, are extremists.

There are others who are ready to acknowledge that there is a place for dogma; it belongs to the study of the theologian, the den of the philosopher, the schoolroom where professor and student meet, the library of the minister; but it has no place in the pulpit toward which worn and wearied mortals look on Sunday morning for a guiding and a healing word amid the temptations and tribulations of the crowded and bewildering days.

The time has come when dogma is everywhere spoken against. Do not the novelists go out of their way to sneer at it? Some of their brightest things are said in disparagement of it. Magazine writers toss it aside with a superior smile as though it belonged to the pile of exploded superstitions. The editors and reporters tear the doctrines and creeds into tatters and twit the minister on the fact that the world is interested no longer in his dogmas. Lords and ladies of high society say with supercilious disdain that they care nothing at all for the "dogmas" of the church. The unbelievers and freethinkers grow furious in the presence of these dogmas and pour out upon them the vials of their wrath, trampling them beneath their feet as the muddy sediment of a stream of superstition, black crystals of bigotry and hate. Tennyson has sketched the typical man of to-day in his lines : —

> "I take possession of man's mind and deed;
> I care not what the sects may brawl;
> I sit as God holding no form of creed,
> But contemplating all."

Now there is nothing new in the fact that the world is opposed to Christian dogma, for it has been so from the beginning. Ever since the days of Saul of Tarsus the dogmas of the Christian church have seemed to one type of men a stumbling-block and to another type of men they have been sheer foolishness. The novel feature of the present situation is that the disparagement of dogma has been taken up by members of the Christian church. Christian authors of Christian volumes speak contemptuously of creeds. The president of a well-known college begins a book with the assertion that the current creed of Christendom is a chaos of contradictions. Christian editors of Christian papers do not hesitate to speak of doctrines as though they were matters of slight concern. Christian men and Christian women and Christian scholars say openly that they do not care for doctrinal preaching, and with the crowd they shout, "Away with your dogmas!" Here and there you will find a preacher who, yielding to the Zeitgeist, falls in with the prevailing fad and rails against dogma too. Dogma is "a monster of such frightful mien, as to be hated needs but to be seen." Some men cannot even pronounce the word without an ictus that is acid.

Certainly such a world-wide movement demands careful consideration. No such fashion would ever have taken hold of the hearts of men had there not been powerful reasons. Why is it that there is a tendency nowadays to depreciate the value of dogma?

1. We are living in a new world. The world has been recreated within seventy-five years. There is a new atmosphere, a new temper, a new perspective, a new viewpoint, a new emphasis, new instruments, new apparatus; all the old horizons of knowledge have disappeared, new worlds have swum into our ken, and a desolating humility has fallen on a large section of the Christian world. Our fathers lived in a much smaller world than ours. They could close every sentence with a period; we are obliged to use the interrogation point. For a generation min-

isters have been repeating in the pulpit : —

> "Our little systems have their day,
> They have their day and cease to be,
> They are but broken lights of Thee,
> And thou, O Lord, art more than they.
>
> "We have but faith, we cannot know,
> For knowledge is of things we see.
> And yet we trust it comes from Thee,
> A beam in darkness, let it grow."

This has been the sentiment of some of
the boldest spirits, while many more intense and more earnest have been driven
to exclaim : —

> "What am I?
> An infant crying in the night —
> An infant crying for the light —
> And with no language but a cry."

In the presence of the immeasurable
spaces and the illimitable forces which
modern science has disclosed, many a
heroic spirit has prostrated itself in the
dust, saying, in answer to all the questions
which religion suggests : " I do not know !
I do not know !" In an age so largely
ruled by the agnostic spirit, it seems out

of place to be dogmatic. Who can be certain in a world where so many men are doubtful? Dogma seems to be an anachronism in our modern life. It is a mark of culture to speak in hesitant and apologetic phrases. With men all around us all at sea it becomes us to hold our opinions also in suspense. To be certain or to know is to get ourself written down a prig.

2. With the new world have come new problems, and these problems seem to be beyond the reach of dogma. Steam and electricity have created a new industrial world. Populations are massing themselves more and more in colossal cities. All our social problems have been multiplied enormously. How to live together — this is the problem of our day. In the rush and push and strife of modern city life there is so much injustice, so much dishonesty, so much cruelty, so much suffering; lust and drunkenness and greed create such terrible tragedies that

religious men are saying, "We must grapple with these awful problems; we must front these pressing perils and let the dogmas go." And so men are building institutional churches and parish houses and college settlements, and philanthropic agencies are multiplied and extended. Every one nowadays believes in institutions which deal directly with the social wants and needs of men. Money is being poured out like water to feed the hungry, to clothe the naked, and to teach the fingers of the ignorant ways of earning bread, and to this grand work many a man goes jauntily forward, saying, "I believe in social service; let the dogmas go."

3. The new age is irenic. The past has been filled with controversy and contention, with bitterness and war. When we read the awful record the head grows faint and the heart sick. The spirit of our times cries out: Let us have peace. Let us forget the points on which we

differ and think only on the points in which we all agree. Let all the evangelical churches come together and let the Unitarians come in too, and let the Jews come in also, and let us receive also the disciples of ethical culture — let us throw away the dogmas on which we differ, and let us think henceforth and forever only of the things on which we can agree. This means, of course, throwing overboard the distinctive dogmas of the Christian religion — but let them go, if only by casting them away we can have peace. Our good nature extends even to the ends of the earth. We are no longer the critics of the Oriental religions. We are willing to admit that Confucianism and Buddhism and Mohammedanism and Shintoism are all earnest strivings of the human spirit after God; that they all have in them many beautiful and noble sentiments and precepts, and why should not the followers of all the religions of the earth get together and sit at one another's feet, culling out the things upon which they are all agreed, and out of these constructing the one universal and final religion ? This means, of course, letting the distinctive dogmas of the Christian religion go — but why not let them go if we can have a world-wide peace ? So many men are saying.

4. The value of dogma as a dynamic is becoming increasingly doubtful. Ralph Waldo Emerson threw over the dogmas of the church one after the other, but he remained a saint to the end of his days. One of the most orthodox of all evangelical preachers, Father Taylor, declared that he had never known so good a Christian as Ralph Waldo Emerson. If Ralph Waldo Emerson could get on without dogma, why should not all men be able to do the same ? Only recently a writer stated in the *Independent* that decadence in church attendance causes no decadence in morals, that many of the best people she knows no longer care to

go to church; and in order to prove her
contention she cited the fact that the
leader of the reform movement in New
York City never goes to church. Christmas morning of last year an editorial
writer in one of the New York dailies
said that while the incarnation to many
minds had passed from the realm of faith
to the region of poetic imagination, nevertheless the idealism of Christmas remains.
The fact that the Christian spirit seems
to abide after the Christian dogmas have
been denied is leading increasing numbers
of people to feel that we can safely
dispense with the dogmatic features of
Christianity, keeping only its beautiful
spirit.

To many minds the virgin birth is
passing from the realm of dogma to the
realm of fancy — let it pass, — it is a
lovely picture and has done the world immeasurable good. The miracles of Jesus
are passing from the realm of fact to
the realm of myth, but let them pass, —

they have done the world a service. The resurrection of Jesus is passing from the realm of history to the realm of halluci- nation, but let it pass, — it has helped men to believe that all men rise. The incar- nation is passing from the realm of faith to the realm of imagination — but let it go, — we should praise the men who were able to entertain so poetic an idea. And so men are throwing away the virgin birth, the miracles, the resurrection, the trin- ity, the incarnation, redemption through Christ's blood, the new birth, heaven, hell, and saying, the Sermon on the Mount is enough. Others, bolder still, say the Golden Rule is sufficient — give us this and we have all we need.

5. In our crowded city life there seems to be no time or place for dogma. A city picks up a man Monday morning, drives him like a slave through the week, throws him into Sunday jaded and wrecked. If the man can get away from his work at night, he goes to some banquet and listens

to speeches that are facetious and witty. On Sunday he is so jaded and fagged that he says, Give me a little good music, and for heaven's sake make the sermon short. In many cases the good-natured preacher obeys, and the Christians of our large cities are not getting the instruction which their fathers received. The children in many cases grow up to be ignorant of the creed of the church, and when they go to college are discovered to be as ignorant of the scriptures as though they were Hottentots. Men and women nourished in orthodox households are ready to be swept along by Dowieism, esoteric Buddhism, Christian Science, or any other insanity or delusion of the hour. It was noted by many that the man whose name stood at the head of the list of the supporters of the beautiful new Christian Science Church on Central Park West was the son of one of the most illustrious of the Presbyterian families of that city.

The false Christs of our day get their

devotees, not from the world, but from the churches of evangelical Christendom. Possibly there never has been a time when there have been so many and such subtle temptations to reduce the Christian religion to an ethical code. Never have there been so many reverent and distinguished and religious men willing to do that as just now. Give us the surface facts. Give us a quick lunch, cries the pew, and the pulpit with alacrity obeys.

I ask you to look at two facts. The first fact is that through a larger part of the Christian world there is a spiritual deadness which is appalling. Our English brethren when they visit us go home and talk about us, and this is what they say about American preachers. They say we are a very bright and learned set, we are intensely intellectual, we know a lot of things, but we are not spiritual, — we are lacking in spiritual passion. If we are to believe what we read in the papers, certainly the churches of America are lacking in enthusiasm and fervor. The motions are still gone through with, but the fires of enthusiasm have died down. A few hopeful souls still tell us there is to be a revival, but the revival has not yet arrived. Masses of our population have drifted out of reach of the church. Those who attend religious services are allowing their church-going to become increasingly desultory and spasmodic. No one who knows the world as it is to-day in its temper and its inmost spirit can deny that it is skeptical and cold, either altogether indifferent to or furiously antagonistic to the dogmas of the Christian faith. Our first fact, then, is a wide-spread spiritual desolation. We publish beautiful and elaborate social programs, but for some reason we cannot carry them out. We have ink, but lack power.

The second fact is a decadence in doctrinal preaching. I suppose the fact that there has been such decadence would hardly be denied by any one. Surely the dogmas of the Christian church are not presented to the people with anything like the clearness, the coherency, or the passion with which they were presented to people fifty years ago. In many a Christian pulpit the dogmas have been slowly disappearing. Occasionally a man stands up and boldly says: "We leave the cross behind us, but let us guard the sacred fire; we cast off dogma, but we keep enthusiasm. Let the old statements go. The incarnation—let it be not special but general, all men are begotten of God. Redemption — let it be merged in the thought of continuous creation. The atonement — let us make it a universal law." Such a man gets into the papers, creates a wide-spread commotion, goes up like a rocket, and comes down like a stick. That is not the kind of heretic of whom we need be afraid in our day and generation. The insidious heretic of our day is the man who quietly drops dogma out of his preaching and says nothing about it. Robert Louis Stevenson was right when he said that the damning sins are the sins of omission. That is what Jesus himself said.

And however it may be with other men, surely the damning sins of preachers are the sins of omission. It is not the things which a minister does, but the things which he does not do which carry him to perdition. A minister in our day can get on very well without dogma. Books are numerous and cheap, and he has a mass of poetry and a mass of fiction and a mass of science and a mass of sociology from which it is possible for him to draw. He can give his sermon the Christian atmosphere and let a stream of Christian sentiment trickle through its paragraphs and keep to the front the Christian ethical ideals, without even so much as once referring to those fundamental dogmas by which the church of

God lifted the Roman Empire off its hinges, and turned the stream of the centuries into a new channel. There is a vast mass of preaching which is not dogmatic. These, then, are the two facts: There is wide-spread spiritual desolation and wide-spread indifference to dogma. Is there a connection between these two facts? I think there is.

And so I stand here to enter a plea for dogma in preaching. There is a place for it, and its place is the foremost place. The man who would be a great preacher is the man who keeps dogma at the front.

1. Let us ask ourselves first of all what dogma is. We cannot do better than to accept the definition of Dr. James Orr, and say that dogma is doctrine clearly stated and ecclesiastically sanctioned. If this be a correct definition, then certainly everybody must believe in Dogma. Sabattier is right when he says that a religion without doctrine is a thing essentially contradictory. And Harnack is not mistaken

when he asserts that Christianity without
dogma, without a clear expression of its
content, is inconceivable. If the intellect
has anything at all to do with a man's religion, if the first great commandment is,
"Thou shalt love the Lord thy God with
all thy heart and soul and *mind* and
strength," then we must think to be genuinely religious, and our thought must be
worked out to clearness and coherency.
And when thus worked out and sanctioned
by the body of believers, it is Christian
dogma.

2. Dogmatic teaching has always been
a source of power. No men have ever
left their mark upon this world who have
not had a definite and clean-cut creed.
Men often talk about the scientific spirit
who do not know what the scientific spirit
is. Science is as dogmatic as the church
was in the mediæval ages. Science has
her creed, and its articles are clear and
definite. The universality of law, the universality of gravitation, the indestructibility

of matter, the conservation of energy, organic evolution, the age of ice, the undulatory nature of light, — these are articles of her creed which she repeats in all her temples, and which she proclaims as one having authority. It is because she has a creed and because she speaks dogmatically that she has filled the modern world with her wonders.

The high priests of science are all of them without exception dogmatists. Tyndall, Huxley, Spencer, and all the rest of them have been as dogmatic as the apologists of the second century were. That has been characteristic of all the mightiest opponents of the Christian church. They have all had a creed and been able to meet the faith of the Christian church by clear and coherent dogmas. We are living in a scientific age, and men demand above all things else clearness, coherency, definiteness. What a tragedy it is that when science is speaking in such clear and positive tones, so many of the

preachers of the Gospel should be speaking
with hesitant voices and blowing the bugle
with a sound so uncertain that men do not
know whether or not to prepare for battle.

What the men in our theological seminaries need most of all is a thorough ground-
ing in theology. Men in a scientific age
want science; theology is the science of
God. If some men are not ashamed to give
their life to the study of the science of the
stars, and others to the study of the science
of flowers, and others to the science of
rocks, and others to the science of bugs,
shame on the Lord's anointed if they are
ashamed to give themselves to the continuous and passionate study of the science
of the Eternal. It is calamitous that in an
age filled with vast confusions and multitudinous speculations so many ministers
of the Gospel should be capable of nothing
but clouded phrases and declarations that
are lacking in the music of final and incon-
trovertible truth. When we are met on
every side by ideas as sharp as lances and

solid as spears, we cannot conquer with hands filled with mist or with mush.

3. One of the mightiest forces of our times is socialism. This is a force which men have already learned to fear, and with which the world is bound to reckon by and by. Karl Marx was the greatest dogmatist which Germany has produced within the last hundred years. He had ideas and he thought them out to clearness, and he stated them in language which burns like a thousand torches, and he has kindled all over the world fires that are burning like subterranean furnaces down deep in the hot souls of men. In the world of socialism there are heroisms and self-abnegations and willingness to suffer, and idealisms which remind one of the days of the apostolic church. With such passionate intensity of devotion and such lofty dreams of the future that shall be, I do not wonder that socialism is looked upon with alarm, and that many socialists are hated with the same fear as

the followers of the crucified Nazarene
were hated two thousand years ago.

4. One of the colossal facts of Christian history is Roman Catholicism. Her
victories are amazing. Her power is stupendous. She has retained her grip upon
the minds and consciences of men through
the storms and changes of more than a
thousand years, and that grip is not yet
broken. She has done it because she has
been from first to last dogmatic. She has
a few ideas which are as clear as crystal
and which she builds up in the minds of
men by patient teaching through the
generations. One of those dogmas is the
dogma of the church. The church is a
divine institution intrusted with the right
to guide and rule the hearts and homes of
men. The second is the dogma of transubstantiation, the dogma that God is
actually present on the altar in the sacrifice of the mass. These two dogmas cannot be questioned by any faithful Catholic
anywhere on the earth. They are taught

in all languages, and without a quiver in
the voice of the instructing priest ; and
because those dogmas are taught and
accepted, nearly three hundred thousand
Roman Catholics on the little island of
Manhattan travel to the house of prayer
every Sunday morning in the early hours,
when Protestants are too tired to get out
of bed, — over twice as many as all the
Protestant church-goers put together, notwithstanding the Protestant population
outnumbers that of the Roman Catholic.
And all this is made possible by the per-
sistent, patient, everlasting teaching of
dogmas.

Protestantism in her origin was also dogmatic. Martin Luther was born a Roman
Catholic, was educated by the Catholic
church, spent years in a Roman Catholic
monastery. He was not afraid of dogma,
and by means of his dogma of justification by faith, he tore Germany from the
grip of the Pope and shook the civilized
world.

What more dogmatic preachers have ever lived than the Presbyterians of Scotland and the Congregationalists of New England? By this dogmatic preaching both countries were lifted to thrones of power, and are known in history as seats of the mighty. Stalwart thinkers of God's truth, they did not hesitate to express it in language which gripped the consciences of men. It is the glory of the Reformed branches of Protestantism, and the feature in their life which makes my heart rejoice is that from the days of John Calvin down to the present generation their leaders have everywhere and always presented a compact body of truth, which has passed like iron into the blood of men. The doctrine of divine sovereignty thought out to clearness and consistency, even though overdeveloped on one side to the verge of cruelty, will bring men nearer to God than will the idea of the divine fatherhood expressed in vague and wandering phrases by minds which have not thought out

what divine parenthood necessitates and
implies.

The mightiest Protestant church of our
modern world is the Methodist. Methodism owes its power to a dogma. It was on
a certain evening in the month of May, in
the year 1738, that John Wesley, attending a religious service in London, while
listening to the exposition of one of St.
Paul's letters, felt his heart strangely
warmed. The fire that was kindled that
night in John Wesley's heart started a
spiritual conflagration which put an end to
the age of ice. On both sides the sea a
dead church was brought to life again by
the preaching of men whose lips had been
touched with a coal from off God's altar,
and who had learned by their own experience that it is possible for a man to be
born from above. "Ye must be born
again;" that is preëminently the dogma
of Methodism.

As it has been the last four hundred
years so it was at the beginning. The apol-

ogists of the second and third centuries were stalwart and uncompromising dogmatists. How easy it would have been for Ignatius and Polycarp and Justin Martyr and the rest of them to have said, We will let the dogmas go; all we desire is that men should be good. But no, they chose rather to die than forego the joy of bearing testimony to the fact that Christ died and rose again. The world was full of specious philosophies, and men were going up and down the lands teaching in elegant and rhetorical phrases the beauty of being good. Vast errors were abroad, protean in shape and cyclopean in power, and these followers of Jesus might have avoided controversy and saved themselves from the stake if they had only been willing to forget the things on which they differed from other men and dwell upon the things on which all good men were agreed. It was the dogmas of the Christian faith which brought them to the fire and opened the gates of heaven.

Moreover, the new preaching of Christianity with Christian dogma eliminated does not seem to be working well. Never have preachers preached so many sermons on the brotherhood of man, and never has that phrase been so often on human lips as within the last fifty years, and yet never since our republic was founded has race hatred burned with greater intensity than it is burning now; never have labor and capital been farther apart, and never has the chasm between rich and poor, high and low, cultivated and ignorant, been wider and deeper; never have the unchurched masses been more indifferent to the church than to-day. Applied Christianity has been our theme; but alas, we have had too little Christianity to apply.

It begins to look as though there must be some fallacy in the argument that all we want is the words of Jesus. Again and again the changes have been rung on the thesis: "Let us take the words of Jesus and let us shape our life by them. Men will never agree upon the dogmas of the church, but upon the words of Jesus all good men are at one. No matter who he was, how he came, or how he went, what he said was beautiful and good. Let us live his life and obey his word, no matter whence he came." It all sounds plausible enough, but when analyzed it is nothing but the talk of fools, for only fools take up the thoughts and follow the commands of strangers, not caring who the strangers are. If one commands me to go and preach his gospel, and if necessary lay down my life in the doing of it, I want to know first of all who he is and whether all power has been granted unto him both in heaven and on earth.

The first question which meets a man who thinks is, Who is Jesus — is he mere man, apparition, chimera, emanation, deceiver, demigod, or God's only begotten Son who "for us men and for our salvation came down from heaven, and was incarnate by the Holy Ghost of the Virgin Mary and was made man"? Who is he? Has the church any clean-cut answer to that question? Is it possible that she has lived her life and done her work for two thousand years and still is all at sea in regard to the person of the one she counts her Lord? If she has a clean-cut conception of who and what he is, then that is dogma, and the dogma of Christ's person becomes the center of all effective and truly Christian preaching.

The words of Jesus are indeed important, but chiefly because of the light they throw on Jesus' person. Take his words as so many ethical precepts and try to plant them in the stony hearts of men, and egregious and tragic failure is inevitable. No such blunder was committed by the apostles. They knew the words of Jesus, but they did not rely upon them for the conversion of the world. It is remarkable that Peter uses hardly any of the words of Jesus in his letters. Neither does John, neither does James. Even Paul quotes him only twice, and then to the extent of scarcely a dozen words. " I am determined to know Christ, not his parables or his discourses, his maxims or his speeches, but the Lord himself who loved me and gave himself for me."

Paul's one ambition was to know *him*, and the power of his resurrection, and the fellowship of his suffering being made conformable unto his death. It is Christ who is the hope of glory. It is Christ in whom we can do all things. For him to live is Christ, and to die is gain, because death will tighten the union between his soul and Christ. It is not the words of Jesus which Paul treasures and extols, but the life that is hid with Christ in God. It is not the words of Jesus, but the dogma of the incarnation which is the center of Paul's theology and the crown and glory of all his preaching. Harnack is fallacious when in the *Contemporary Review* of April, 1903, he says, "It is more important to ponder on the words, 'If ye love me, ye will keep my commandments,' and to order our lives in conformity with them than to press the inscrutable and venerable formulas."

Yes, but to order our lives in conformity with the words of Jesus — ah, there's the rub! Unless we die with him how can we rise with him, unless we suffer with him how can we reign with him, and what will induce us to suffer with him except our belief in him as one who, existing "in the form of God, counted not the being on an equality with God, a thing to be grasped, but emptied himself, taking the form of a servant, being made in the likeness of men; and, being found in fashion as a man, he humbled himself, becoming obedient unto death,— yea, the death of the cross."

"Religion," says Matthew Arnold, is "morality touched with emotion, lit up and enkindled and made much more powerful by emotion." Yes, but how is one to get the emotion? Whence is it to come?

Not from beautiful precepts such as "Love your enemies," or "Love your neighbor as yourself," or "If you would save your life, lose it," but from the loving heart of a person who becomes the life of our life and the love of our love. Men are not saved by words, but by a person. What they need is a restored relationship to God. Only as we can persuade them that God is in Christ reconciling the world to himself does the fire burn on the altar, and human brotherhood become possible. Every man of power in the pulpit from Ignatius down to Dwight L. Moody has been mighty in his dogmatism. Seizing clean-cut definite truths which have received the sanction of the body of believers, they have so pressed these upon the hearts of their hearers as to make them the power of God unto salvation to every one willing to believe.

When, therefore, a good ministerial brother in the *Outlook* asks, "Is not belief in the unceasing presence of a divine intelligence active in power and boundless in love enough?" the answer is No! It is Christ and him crucified which forms the preacher's message, and leaving Christ out he abdicates the high position to which he has been called. A preacher must have impulse, power, and passion,— these three, and all these three come only in fullest measure from the cross. The incarnation, the trinity, redemption through the blood of Christ, immortality through union with the Son of God, the Christian church, Christ's body,— these are not golden-tinted exhalations floating on the surface of the great river of human speculation, bubbles to be toyed with for a season and blown to nothingness by the gales of a scientific age; they are outcroppings of the Eternal granite on which the universe is built. Blessed is the preacher who plants his feet on these! A pulpit built on these is built on rock, and no matter how the winds may blow or the rains descend, that pulpit will stand forever!

When we open our New Testament

we are ushered at once into the presence of a company of dogmatists. Not one of them is vague or limp or gelatinous. Listen to Simon Peter preaching to the people of Jerusalem, "There is no name under heaven which is given among men wherein ye must be saved." Oh, the narrowness of the man! The temper of Peter was the temper of all. Listen to the man who lay with his head on Jesus' bosom in the upper chamber at the last supper: "Who is the liar but he that denieth that Jesus is the Christ? He is antichrist that denieth the Father and the Son. Whosoever denieth the Son hath not the Father." And Paul is like John. Listen to him as he writes to the Galatians, "Though an angel from heaven preached any other Gospel to you than that which we have preached unto you, let him be accursed." And fearing that some one in the church might think that he was heated and hasty he says, "Now let me say that again."

Wherever Paul went he preached dogma. He says to the Roman world, "I am not ashamed of the Gospel." There were a thousand reasons why he might have been ashamed of it. The idea that a dead Jew should come to life again, get up out of his grave, and by and by float upward into the clouds was apparently about the most silly and preposterous story that one man could tell to another. And this was the story that St. Paul had to tell, and he says, I am not ashamed of it. Why, Paul, were you not ashamed? Because it is the power of God unto salvation to every one that believes. Whenever he writes a letter he puts dogma first and ethics second. The first eleven chapters of his letter to the Romans are dogmatic. After he has laid down his dogmas he is ready for his ethics. "I beseech you therefore, brethren, by the mercies of God — " Or take the fifteenth chapter of 1 Corinthians — that immortal argument for the resurrection.

Round by round he climbs until at the top he shouts, "Therefore, my beloved brethren." It is only when we stand on the dogma of the resurrection that we have power sufficient to enable us to be immovable, and to always abound in the work of the Lord. Or take his letter to the Ephesians; the first three chapters are dogmatic. After the dogmas are stated, "I therefore beseech you that ye walk worthy of the vocation wherewith ye are called." Or take his letter to the Philippians, "Let this mind be in you which was also in Christ Jesus, who, being in the form of God, thought it not robbery to be equal with God, made himself of no reputation, and took upon him the form of a servant." It is after looking once more at the face of Christ that he ventures to tell the Philippians what they ought to do.

When he wants money he takes his stand upon dogma. "You remember the grace of our Lord Jesus, how that he was rich, yet for your sakes he became poor, that ye through his poverty might be rich." He did not ask people to give money because it was right, or because people were suffering, or because it was a fine thing ethically for them to do. He stood on the incarnation whenever he asked for money. Or take his letter to the Colossians: "If ye be risen with Christ, seek those things which are above. Set your affection on things above, not on things on the earth, for ye are dead, and your life is hid with Christ in God." See how he buttresses his ethics both in front and behind by glowing visions of the risen Christ. That is the way to preach. No other kind of preaching is really Christian preaching.

Where did the apostles get this dogmatic temper and this dogmatic habit? They got it from the Lord himself. He is the crowned dogmatist of history. Even the stupid people of his day could see that he was unlike all other teachers in that he

spoke as one having authority. " It hath
been said by them of old time — but I say
unto you —   Other men have said this and
that, but I say unto you — " He lifted
himself above prophet, priest, and law-
giver, above the exalted head of Moses
himself.   And lo, before men were aware
of what he was doing, he had seated himself on the throne of God.   " Many will
say to me in that day, Lord, Lord, and
then will I say unto them, I never knew
you."

To his disciples in the upper chamber he
said, " As my Father hath sent me, even
so send I you."   And what he said to them
he says to us.   Before the cloud received
him from their sight, he said : " All power
is given unto me, both in heaven and on
earth — Go, therefore ! "   He stood on
dogma in issuing his commands.   Without
the dogma we have not the disposition or
the power to go.   I do not believe that a
man has the right to preach the Gospel
of the Son of God unless he can preach

dogmatically. It seems to me that the preacher is bound to know some things, and to know them thoroughly. I do not believe a man has a right to preach who cannot speak the great truths of the Christian revelation in accents which do not waver and with an emphasis that burns with fervent heat.

In saying all this I would not imply that everything is fixed down to the minutest details. I would leave large spaces in which the human mind may work. Our fathers made the blunder of being certain on too many things. There is room for agnosticism within the area of well-defined limits. Christianity has its mysteries. Life's horizon is robed in mists, and the religion of the man of Galilee does not dissipate the mists. We see through a glass darkly, and no matter how much we know we know only in part. "It doth not yet appear what we shall be." In the heavens of the Christian world there are clouds of golden glory into which we look awestruck and with eyes filled with wonder; but there are vast ranges of mountain truth whose glowing tops stand out sharp cut and glorious against the sky. These mountain ranges are the mysteries which were hidden from the foundation of the world and which have been revealed to us by God in Jesus Christ his Son. There are some things which we know, and the things which we know are the things which we must preach. Do we not know that God so loved the world that he gave his only begotten Son that whosoever believeth in him might not perish, but have eternal life? Do we not know that Christ died for our sins and rose again for our justification? Mists hang heavy all around the horizon, but there is everlasting granite beneath our feet. Can we not sing:—

"There is a fountain filled with blood,
    Drawn from Immanuel's veins;
And sinners, plunged beneath that flood,
    Lose all their guilty stains."

Can we not say with the Christian poet: —

> " Oh, 'twas love, 'twas wondrous love,
>   The love of God to me.
> It brought my Saviour from above
>   To die on Calvary."